PASTOR AND PRESIDENT
Reflections of a Lutheran Churchman

David W. Preus

Lutheran University Press
Minneapolis, Minnesota

PASTOR AND PRESIDENT
Reflections of a Lutheran Churchman
David W. Preus

Library of Congress Cataloging-in-Publication Data

Preus, David W.
    Pastor and president : reflections of a Lutheran churchman / David W. Preus.
        p. cm.
    ISBN-13: 978-1-932688-64-1 (alk. paper)
    ISBN-10: 1-932688-64-1 (alk. paper)
    1. American Lutheran Church (1961-1987) 2. Preus, David W. I. Title.
    BX8047.7.P74 2011
    284.1'31~dc23
                            2011033684

Lutheran University Press, PO Box 390759, Minneapolis, MN 55439
Manufactured in the United States of America

CONTENTS

FOREWORD

David Preus was one of the significant leaders of the Lutheran church during the second half of the twentieth century. Ordained in 1950 into the parish ministry of the Evangelical Lutheran Church, he served congregations until 1973, during the last five years of which he also served as vice president of the American Lutheran Church. He became president of the American Lutheran Church in 1973, serving in that position until he retired in 1987.

Four themes dominated his career. He had a passionate commitment to the local congregation as the focus of the church's ministry and work. He emphasized evangelism as the center of the church's work. He worked untiringly for the unity of all of Lutheranism. And from the beginning of his ministry, he sought to bring the American Lutheran Church into full participation in the ecumenical movement.

Those principles, his commitment to justice, together with his position as president of a major U.S. denomination were factors that contributed to Preus' prominent role on the world stage for more than twenty years.

As a pastor in Minneapolis and chair of the Minneapolis School Board, he was involved in the civil rights struggles of the late 1960s. He marched with Martin Luther King Jr. and was a local leader in an attack on poverty and urban blight.

Within five years of ordination, Preus was one of the chief leaders in bringing the denomination into full membership in the World Council of Churches. He was an early consultant with South African Bishop Desmond Tutu. Preus' subsequent activity through the World Council of Churches brought the injustices of apartheid to the attention of U.S. churches, and thus he played a key role in creating the pressure that brought the end of apartheid.

His leadership positions on troubling issues brought him national attention. On a couple occasions Preus was called to Camp David to serve as a consultant to President Jimmy Carter. He has teamed with former Vice President Walter Mondale in support of local initiatives.

In his many visits to churches in the Soviet bloc countries, Preus met with the cabinet level church relations officers, making a strong pitch for religious freedom. His strong support of churches in Eastern Europe played a significant role in their internal push for the fall of the Iron Curtain. Preus was named vice-moderator of the 1982 Moscow Peace Conference sponsored by the Russian Orthodox Church.

Preus was instrumental in bringing the annual Nobel Peace Prize Forum to a cluster of Upper Midwest Lutheran colleges.

As a church president committed to Lutheran unity, he took an unpopular stand in the mid-1980s merger negotiations between the American Lutheran Church and the Lutheran Church in America. He insisted that organic structure was not necessary to demonstrate unity.

Preus' low-key, modest account is a primary source for a little-known piece of American church history and slices of world history.

> Dr. Lloyd Svendsbye
> Former Vice President, the American Lutheran Church
> President Emeritus, Luther Seminary
> President Emeritus, Augustana College

INTRODUCTION

A career as a pastor was not something I considered during my first twenty-five years of life. I had no inclination to become a pastor. Though raised in a covey of Evangelical Lutheran Church/American Lutheran Church pastors—my father, two brothers, a brother-in-law—and though loving and admiring all of them, I did not even consider becoming a pastor. My interests were elsewhere. During my Luther College years I was an avid athlete, and I prepared to become a coach and teacher. Before I could begin that career I was called to serve in the U.S. Army. I served for more than three years during World War II, mostly in Washington, D C., then in the Philippine Islands, and at the end of the war in Japan. During those army years coaching lost its luster, and I decided my future would be as a lawyer. In the fall of 1946, newly discharged from the army, I began studies at the University of Minnesota Law School.

While law school was demanding and occupied most of my time, other activities became important in my life. At Lutheran Students' Association I met students whose Christian faith and understanding was much deeper than my own. I became conscious of how little I knew about Christian theology. I roomed in the home of my cousin, good friend, and school mate, Jack Preus, a pastor of the Evangelical Lutheran Church (ELC), who was finishing his doctoral work in classics at the university. Jack and his brother, Robert, were in the process of leaving the ELC for a more theologically conservative church body. They talked theology incessantly, and I often listened. During that same year I visited often with my pastor brothers Christian and Nelson and brother-in-law Alvin Rogness, and was fascinated by the way they and their spouses enjoyed life in the parish.

By year's end I was planning how I could become a much more knowledgeable follower of Christ. The need for a personal working theology became more and more urgent. I did not want to become only a loyal church member. I longed to know how to articulate the faith that was in me. I began to think a year at nearby Luther Seminary would be a year well spent. However, I discovered that Luther accepted only those who believed themselves called by God to be a parish pastor. I was aware of no such call and put aside the seminary option.

In the fall of 1947, I was in the law school registering for my second year when I suddenly decided to ask the seminary authorities if they would accept me for a year's study without any further commitment. I immediately took the streetcar to the seminary and proposed to President Gullixson that I be allowed to spend a year at the seminary. To my surprise and pleasure the answer was affirmative. Seminary classes had already begun, and the next day I joined the first-year class.

It took only a semester at the seminary for me to believe I was called by God to be a pastor. When I became acquainted with my new classmates I discovered how many different ways God summoned people to be pastors.

The Lutheran Confessions have been at the center of my faith and life ever since the start of my pastoral life. They point to what is essential, the heart and body of the Christian faith. Such Lutheran confessional items as the creative power of God, justification by grace through faith in Jesus, the work of the Spirit of God, the universal priesthood of believers, the two kingdoms, living with paradox, and the call to a servant life were always providing guidance as I sought to order my life and provide responsible leadership.

My first pastoral service was in Brookings, South Dakota (1950-1951), where I served as assistant pastor at First Lutheran Church. It was also where I met, courted, and married Ann Madsen, my wonderful, life-long spouse and partner in ministry. Following a term of study at Edinburgh University in Scotland, I accepted a call to Trinity Lutheran Church in Vermillion, South Dakota. Both Brookings and Vermillion housed state universities, and the congregations were challenging mixes of farmers, small business operators, professional people, laborers, and university faculty, staff, and students.

Following a year as Lutheran campus pastor at the University of Minnesota (1956-1957), I became pastor of University Lutheran Church of Hope in Minneapolis, Minnesota. It was a great time to be a pastor at Hope Church. Church membership and participation were at a peak. Worship services were packed. Children flooded the Sunday schools. Youth work flourished. University students attended church in droves.

The Korean War and the early stages of the Cold War kept American people uneasy, but comparatively it was a time of peace and prosperity. That brief interlude soon ended.

The 1960s brought turmoil. Civil rights battles brought violence and destruction to city streets. Cold War threats of nuclear disaster were a constant worry. The assassinations of President Kennedy, civil rights leader Martin Luther King Jr., and U.S. Attorney General Robert Kennedy shocked and shook the nation. The disastrous Vietnam War with its hated military draft divided the citizenry into opposing factions. Disillusion, anger, and rebellion swept through the ranks of young people and brought in their wake rampant drug use, sexual license, burning of draft cards, protest parades, public building sit-ins, anti-institutionalism, angry denunciations of civic leaders. It was all gathered up somehow in the mantra, "Make love, not war." Churches were inevitably involved along with the rest of society. These events provide the public backdrop both for my personal vocational history and the story of the American Lutheran Church (ALC).

The possibility that I might become president of the ALC did not occur to me until I was elected ALC vice president in 1968. At the August 1970 ALC convention Dr. Kent Knutson was elected president and I was re-elected vice president. Kent became seriously ill in the fall of 1972 and died in March of 1973. I was installed as president shortly thereafter.

Twenty years after leaving office as president/presiding bishop of the American Lutheran Church, I determined to do something personally satisfying with the diaries, sermons, reports, speeches, articles, and recollections I had accumulated during my fifteen years (1973-1987) as president/presiding bishop of the ALC. (I will use the title "president" throughout this volume although the term "presiding bishop" became optional during my years in office and became the more widely used title.) Originally my intent was to write only of the fifteen years as president. Once I began writing, however, it seemed impossible to write of those years without frequent reference to the experiences from twenty-three years (1950-1973) as parish pastor. In so many ways service as president seemed an extension of my work in the parish. I understand why the ALC constitution required that the president have experience as a parish pastor. Intimate knowledge of parish life is a necessity for a bishop called to serve many congregations and pastors.

In the pages that follow I will give a very personal report on my years of service as parish pastor and church body president. While I am not attempting to write an ALC history for those years, my vocational life was in service to the American Lutheran Church. Inevitably my very personal story says a great deal about the American Lutheran Church during those years.

Both pastor and president are generalists who, in their calling, face many priorities and must organize them in some coherent way. Seeking to be faithful to the Triune God is the priority for believers. Under that all-encompassing rubric there are sub-priorities that give direction to one's life and work. I claimed four broad priorities in my work as parish pastor and as church body president. They were evangelism, congregations, unity, and justice. All the work of the ALC is subsumed under these four priorities. The first two were obvious priorities from the time I believed myself called to be a pastor. A pastor is first of all a witness to the gospel, the life, teachings, death, resurrection, and lordship of Jesus, faith in whom brings to the believer freedom from sin, death, and the power of Satan. The pastor is called by a congregation to serve as pastor and leader within the congregation and in its ministry beyond the congregational borders. The second two, unity and justice, grew in importance throughout my years of ministry. American religious, political, and cultural worlds were in flux, and divisions were rampant. It became increasingly apparent that both unity and justice are imperative if God is obeyed and humans are to live in peace.

Finding proper church stances that usefully addressed issues of unity and justice was difficult and often contentious. The Lutheran Confessions do not address everything that becomes important. To find and support unity in times of deep division was challenging throughout my years as pastor and president. To discern and address the most critical justice issues in a world where Cold War, poverty, and racism were rampant required careful judgment and great patience with one another. Absolute certainty of rightness was a luxury seldom available.

All four priorities are consistently present in the life of the church and provide guidance for the church in all its life and work. A pastor does not focus on evangelism for a while, then shift to congregational life, and then to unity and justice. The overlaps are constant. One of the priorities might be the particular focus at any time, but the others are simultaneously involved. I will make introductory statements on each of these priorities so that the reader will more easily understand why I thought them particularly central. It will also give me an opportunity to preview the areas of service in which I believed myself called to provide leadership.

Two final introductory notes:

It was tempting to add "joy" as a fifth priority. My first sermon after being installed as ALC president was entitled "Jesus, Justice, Joy." "Rejoice in the Lord always . . . the Lord is at hand" (Philippians 4:4-5) is a strong biblical word that has not been adequately stressed in Lutheran congregations. Martin and Katie Luther, beset with trials, troubles, and threats maintained a marital, home, and church life that provided endless occasions of joy that outshone their times of fear, worry, and depression. Yet American Lutherans did not seem to match the Luthers' experiences of joy or Jesus' words that he had come that our "joy may be full" (John 15:11). Too often our worship services have been slow, stuffy, and even boring. I rejoiced that during my years ALC worship services became increasingly up-beat. I was delighted that a new group of Lutheran hymn writers—John Ylvisaker, Herb Brokering, Marty Haugen, Gracia Grindal, and others—were adding joyous and theologically helpful hymns to the great corpus of hymnody that has blessed the church through the centuries. I hope my personal reflections in these pages will carry overtones of the joy in the gospel that I experienced throughout my years as pastor and president.

The normal duties of pastor and president such as preaching, study, prayer, counseling, setting agendas, addressing conventions and congregations, meeting with boards and committees, making regular stops at ALC seminaries and colleges, seeking every possible way to serve the congregations of the church and the whole human society, and striving to keep the congregations of the church focused on living in unity and doing mission, claimed at least two-thirds of my time. The other one-third of my time was devoted to leadership in ecumenical affairs, the search for unity, and serving the causes of justice and peace. In all of these things I understood myself to be serving the ALC. The chapters that follow are not weighted according to the amount of time spent on various responsibilities. The "normal things" are taken for granted by most church members and do not require lengthy description. Hence I write more about the one-third aspects of my ministry, and less about the two-thirds. It is important for readers to keep this in mind as they assess my reflections.

CHAPTER ONE

AMERICAN LUTHERAN CHURCH PRIORITIES

Evangelism

"God was in Christ reconciling the world to himself" (2 Corinthians 5:19). That, in brief, is the gospel, the good news that people are called to live and to share no matter what the circumstances of life. "Go, make disciples of all nations" (Matthew 28:19) is the follow up for gospel faith. Experiencing and witnessing to the love of God—embodied in the life, teachings, suffering, death, resurrection, and lordship of Jesus—is evangelism and the chief task of the church. Both verbal witness and doing works of love are parts of evangelical outreach. One's vocation as a servant of God at home, in church, at work, in the community, and in all of life is the witness by which God reaches the hearts of others. Vital congregations always know themselves to be a missionary people. The ALC's budgetary makeup was testimony to that fact. Congregations supported missionary efforts of the ALC far more generously than any other portion of church work. The ALC throughout its history had sent large numbers of missionaries to many countries throughout the world. The same was the case on the home scene. Mission pastors were sent to hundreds of U.S. communities to start and grow new congregations of believers. It was the communities of believers in local congregations who were initiating and supporting the ALC missionary outreach.

There is always tension in church life between evangelism and social ministry, even though both are parts of God's charge to believers. The relative attention given one or the other easily causes contention among believers. There was a feeling among many Lutherans that much of Protestantism had become so concentrated on social ministries that their passion for missionary outreach was in doubt. On the other hand were the many who thought that Lutheran people too easily settled for gospel words while ignoring the need for gospel deeds. Tensions become sharper when churches call on the state to offer welfare to needy citizens. The separation of church and state is cited as cause for churches to "stay out of politics." Church bodies have to be judicious and patient when choosing concerns to present to public bodies. Many contemporary issues are not directly addressed by Scripture, and devout Christians can differ. Overwhelming consensus should be present in order for church bodies to take public stances. Individuals, however, should seek what seems to them to be just in current life and then participate in public decision making. I believe the ALC provided responsible leadership for both direct gospel witness and social ministry throughout its life.

Lutheran personal evangelism has been generally low-key. The waves of Lutheran immigrants who formed the first Lutheran churches in the U.S. came from countries with state churches. Christian faith was synonymous with national citizenship. Everybody was considered Christian, so there was no need for evangelism other than the instruction of the young. Circumstances were different in the U.S. There was nothing automatic about membership in the Christian church. Evangelical outreach needed a new start in the U.S. Lutherans generally did not share in the American history of large tent meetings, altar calls, personal public testimony, or aggressive confronting of others for the purpose of conversions. Lutheran evangelism most often has been congregationally oriented, with strong emphasis on Word and Sacrament worship, church schools, confirmation, and adult education combined with acts of justice and mercy aimed at helping the poor. The confidence is that vigorous congregational life will attract the attention and ignite the interest of those outside the church. The ALC always sought ways to increase member participation in personal evangelism, but it remains an ongoing task.

The fact that U.S. Lutherans so often used the term "evangelical" in the names of their church bodies is significant. It declares both the good news of salvation through Christ and the summons to lives of service.

Congregations

The local community of believers is the earthly center of a Christian's faith and life. It is where people are baptized, come to faith, and understand themselves to be members of the church of Christ. It is the basic worshipping center, the learning center, the center for mutual burden bearing, and the center for the missionary life of the church. It is the primary earthly manifestation of the church of Christ.

Serving God through pastoral care of the congregation was first on my mind as I began ordained service. A congregation of believers had called me to serve as pastor, and I looked forward to the endless opportunities to preach and teach the gospel of Christ, administer the sacraments, visit the sick and home bound, be available for confession and counsel, share the joys and sorrows of parishioners, reach out to those who did not yet share the faith, and represent and lead the congregation in serving needs beyond the congregation. Pastoral service to the congregation remained my first priority no matter how much work beyond the congregation increased. I served ELC and ALC congregations as a parish pastor for twenty-three exciting and fulfilling years, and I fully expected and looked forward to remaining a parish pastor the rest of my work life.

My early life as an adult Christian was strongly individual—as is common with many Americans. God was my creator. Christ was my Savior. The Spirit was at work in me. As a beginning pastor I thought almost exclusively in terms of individual salvation. The intensely personal character of faith in God put membership in a congregation in a secondary position, nearly optional in actual practice.

Life as a pastor quickly changed that. Baptism became more than a rite of passage; it became entrance into the congregation and into the great communion of saints, not just to a future heavenly family. The congregation became both the provider of a Word and Sacrament ministry to sustain and deepen personal faith and a community of servants reaching out to others. Faith was more than an individual matter. Increasingly I became aware of the congregation as a burden-sharing community of people who were striving to create unity and justice under God in both church and society. Awareness of the basic character of life in a congregation became central to my own faith and life, a gift I sought to share with others.

Later, as church president it became apparent that strong local congregations are the bedrock for all other expressions of the church. It was always the congregations that determined the strength and seriousness and joy in the ALC's efforts for evangelism, unity, and justice. Missionary sending and support were rooted in the congregations. The far-flung service ministries of the ALC were entirely dependent on the direction and support given by the congregations. The quality of the services the ALC provided for its congregations was totally dependent on congregational support. The strength of the local congregations was reflected in the strength of the ALC.

Because the ALC and its national offices were totally dependent on its member congregations, the ALC national boards and offices were accountable to those congregations. The congregations carried on a vigorous missionary and service ministry through those national offices, and the national offices provided a wide variety of services designed to strengthen the congregations. It was congregational unity and esprit that made the ALC strong in life and work. The ALC was always congregations at work.

Unity

God's call to live in unity is clear (John 17). Paul takes up the theme in his epistle to the Romans: "We, though many, are one body in Christ and individually members of one another" (Romans 12:5). Again in Ephesians readers are admonished that there is "one Lord, one faith, one baptism, one God and Father of us all" (Ephesians 4:5-6). Unity in Christ's body is both a given and a goal. Believers are one in Christ, but expressing that unity is often a difficult task. Human differences and sin tend to pit us against each other in spite of our unity in Christ's body.

On becoming ALC president I saw three immediate needs on the unity front: The first was to deepen the sense of Christian unity among the congregations of the ALC. The second was to seek closer altar and pulpit ties with Christians of other denominations. ALC congregations were increasingly practicing open communion, and the laity were comfortable in all kinds of ecumenical settings. I believed the time had come for the churches to openly express their greater unity in Christ and not be dominated by the lesser, though important, differences. The third was to seek some form of U.S. Lutheran unity that would enable the Lutheran Church–Missouri Synod (LCMS) to join the ALC and the Lutheran Church in America (LCA) in facing the churches' challenges together.

The unity of the congregation is an important matter for pastors. It is a given in terms of faith in Christ, but it requires work to express unity in the often chaotic flux of congregational life. The same is true with respect to a church body and its president. A predecessor president of the ALC, Dr. Fred Schiotz, told me of the broad varieties of people in the ALC and charged me to use the president's office to cement the unity while supporting the variety. The unity of the church was both a present treasure to be claimed and a future reality to be sought.

The unity of Christ's church is experienced primarily in two settings. One is the local fellowship of believers, and the other is the one, holy, catholic, and apostolic church that includes God's people of all times and all places. They are the two expressions of the church that one finds in the Scriptures, and they are the two expressions of the church to which all believers belong. That, to my mind, establishes a priority for the local congregation and the total communion of saints. I write that as one who spent a major share of my ALC presidential life reaching out to and identifying with an "ecclesiastical middle." For me that "middle" included Lutheran conferences, synods, church bodies, the Lutheran Council USA (LCUSA), and the Lutheran World Federation (LWF). It also included local and national organizations and the World Councils of Churches (WCC). Both denominational and ecumenical organizations are expressions of unity and are "church" in that they are gatherings of believers. But they are called into being by the congregations, are dependent on the congregations, and remain accountable to those congregations.

During my years of pastoral service there has been insistence that the disunity of the church is a "scandal" and that the churches must show a "visible" unity. For many believers the "visible" unity of the church is envisioned as requiring organizational uniformity. The presence of several denominationally different congregations in the same community has been viewed as scandalous. The variety of regional, national, or international denominations has been seen as scandalous. The apparent assumption is that the Christian goal is to have one large church organization in order to express the unity.

I have argued that the scandal of disunity is not the fact that we have many different church organizations, but in the self-righteous rejection of each other, angry denunciations of each other, even warring with each other, as well as the refusal to share the Lord's Supper and the rejection of fellowship and cooperation with other Christians.

Of course there are important differences of doctrine and practice within the Christian family, and it does no good to ignore them. Theology is important! Lively discussion and debate is necessary to keep believers focused on God and God's dealings with God's people. Church members need to study the Scriptures, argue for the importance of core doctrines, differ openly when necessary, while at the same time confessing a transcendent unity among those whose ultimate faith is in Christ. Jesus is the "way, the truth, and the life." Christians who affirm that ought to join together at the Lord's table.

Confessional differences as well as geographical, national, linguistic, worship style, and cultural differences may necessitate separate congregations and denominational groupings. It is true that too often Christians have divided because of comparatively minor issues. But to acknowledge that ought not to require a uniformity that seeks to lessen the diversity among God's people.

Christian believers have spent an undue amount of time, energy, and resources in insisting that Christian unity must be expressed in some form of organizational uniformity. The Roman Catholic Church with its tight hierarchical character and insistence that it is the one church to which all Christians should belong is the primary illustration of organizational oneness. However, members of various Protestant and Orthodox congregations also have assumed that membership in the one church of Christ requires the goal of a single organizational expression. There is a strong human sense that unity requires uniformity.

My conviction is that Christian unity should be experienced across geographic, linguistic, historical, and even doctrinal and denominational divides in a unity of reconciled diversity. Such expressed unity may or may not lead to organizational mergers; Christ's work of reconciliation calls for unity but not uniformity. Reconciled diversity contests the view that true unity would automatically eliminate the need for differing denominations. It acknowledges that there is no biblical mandate for how congregations should join together in expressing their unity and in doing the mission of the church. Christian people have to decide what forms are most effective and be willing to change them if grace and wisdom so dictate. The rich diversity in churchly forms and practices cannot be happily and usefully squeezed into a single organization. Theological differences are important. Denominations may be necessary to keep the church from spending its energy introspectively seeking agreement on all doctrines and practice.

My best judgment is that the church's oneness should result in mutual acceptance at the Lord's table of all who confess faith in the Triune God and the lordship of Christ. Heretics would still be heretics; theological study and debate would continue to disclose both deep differences and meaningful agreements. All the differences in culture, language, liturgical practices, and church order would likely continue. Existing church bodies would maintain their current identity while acknowledging their oneness in Christ. It would be messy, but it would be a beginning. The Lord's table ought not be a disciplinary tool with some form of ecclesiastical elite determining who should be there.

Prior to my work as a pastor I had not really thought about a unity that claims the entire cosmos, the whole creation. In the course of my service as parish pastor and church president I became increasingly aware of God's call for the unity of all existence. God's call to love the neighbor and the many admonitions to do good works aims at the creation of a human society with sufficient unity that justice and peace prevails for all people and for the whole creation. Thinking in terms of the unity of the entire human society began for me when the congregation I served extended its ministry in Southeast Minneapolis through a Southeast Minneapolis Planning and Coordinating Committee (SEMPACC). The committee sought to unite all sectors of the community in order that a strong and just human society could exist among a wide variety of believers and unbelievers. Common humanity serving the common good became more than a cliché.

The sense of a global unity became more pronounced for me when involved in the work of the larger church organizations such as the ALC, the Lutheran World Federation, and the World Council of Churches. Efforts to overcome poverty and injustice throughout the world require some sense of commonality in all sectors of human society. The missionary efforts of the Christian churches, while centered in bringing the saving gospel of Christ to people in the far-flung corners of the earth, have also been efforts to bring the whole of existence into a peaceful unity. The churches' medical missions, relief endeavors, and support for indigenous governing structures have been powerful sources for good. The crucial historic role of churches in initiating universal public education required efforts to unite the entire society around a common objective. All such efforts sought the health and unity of the entire community. I was deeply moved by listening to theologian Joseph Sittler as he described the necessity of humans making peace with their "sister nature."

The church at its best has sought earthly unity for all humanity alongside its work for the unity of the church. The goals of the two kinds of unity are not identical, but they do overlap. The unity of the church joins the people of God in an eternal relationship with all believers of all times, together with all the heavenly hosts and a new heaven and earth. The unity of all existence is aimed at a reign of justice and peace for the life of planet Earth. As a leader and representative of the congregations of the ALC, I found myself more and more deeply engaged in supporting efforts to move the whole of society toward unity in the whole of existence. That also will become evident in later parts of this book.

Justice

Justice as a religious term was not on my agenda during my early years. It was not that the Lutheran church of my youth was against pursuit of justice in the wider society, but such efforts were seen as the responsibility of individual Christians in their secular lives. Efforts within the church on behalf of people in poverty were seen as acts of mercy. The connections between injustice and poverty were not given attention. The congregations and the national church body did an immense amount of good in feeding and clothing the poor and in supporting orphans and indigent elderly. No comparable attention was given, for instance, to the injustice of unequal educational opportunity for poor people or housing segregation on the basis of race. Matters of justice were seen as "political" and were to be kept out of congregational life. Justice was the responsibility of the government and the courts. It seemed good for Lutheran congregations to join in doing works of mercy in the secular world, but pursuit of justice was seen as public responsibility and not a central part of Christian discipleship.

To illustrate, as children we learned many Bible passages at home and in church. The passages told us of God's love for us and summoned us to love our neighbors. In Sunday school we gave regular offerings for missionaries and for aid to a wide spectrum of needy people. I look back with gratitude for that grounding. However, I also look back and see that we heard about loving the neighbor by being merciful, but we heard nothing about showing love through doing justice. I had not heard Micah 6:8—"What does God require of you but to do justice, and to love kindness, and to walk humbly with your God?"—among the central Bible passages to remember.

During my young adult years the appearance of Hitler and Stalin and Mussolini made it apparent that to be politically quiescent in the face of massive injustice was not an option for followers of Christ. The relation between doing justice and striving for peace became personally apparent. For me and millions of other Americans it necessitated years of service in the U.S. armed services. The prophetic tradition of Judaism and Christianity with its necessity for religious people to speak and act for justice in the public arena had to be embraced.

In attempting to be a faithful adult disciple of Christ, I had to be an active participant in support of justice. My growing awareness of this necessity became ever more apparent in serving as a parish pastor. The surrounding community of the Minneapolis congregation I served faced major urban neighborhood disruption and decay, and the civil rights movement exploded in America and in our neighborhood following World War II.

The biblical call to love the neighbor by doing justice was a major factor in inspiring both University Lutheran Church of Hope and its pastor to become deeply involved in community organizing and engaging in civil rights activity. The involvement with doing justice in order to establish peace in community, church, nation, and world never left me.

While still a parish pastor I represented the ALC at a White House Consultation on Equal Educational Opportunity. Service on the Minneapolis Board of Education made me very aware of unequal educational opportunity for both children of poverty and of minority races. Subsequently the ALC general convention adopted a resolution calling for governmental action to assure equal educational opportunity. It is illustrative of several areas where the ALC called on national and local governments to address compelling justice issues. The relations between justice and peace are obvious, and the responsibility of the people of God to call for and work for justice is deeply biblical. The separation of church and state was scrupulously observed throughout the ALC.

It will be apparent in this report on my work both as parish pastor and church president that serving God and people through working for justice was a major priority for the congregations I served, for the ALC, and for me personally.

CHAPTER TWO

PARISH PASTOR

Serving Within the Congregation

Service as parish pastor enabled me to know and appreciate the importance of the local congregation and its many facets of life and work. Pastoral service in Brookings and Vermillion, South Dakota, provided experience in America's rural heartland, site of the majority of ALC congregations. Urban experience came from serving as campus pastor at the University of Minnesota and then as pastor of the University Lutheran Church of Hope, a center city Minneapolis congregation.

Since my early years as a pastor I have been convinced that nobody has greater vocational fulfillment than a pastor. I reveled in the many pastoral tasks. The pastor is privileged to preach the gospel again and again but also to bring a blessing from God to parishioners at their moments of greatest joy and greatest sorrow. The pastor's presence is wanted at weddings, baptisms, confirmations, Christmas, Easter, graduations, job promotions, homecomings, and other celebratory occasions. And the pastor's ministry is wanted at times of great distress, unexpected tragedy, suffering, and death. Day after day, in extraordinary times and in ordinary times, the pastor is asked to be God's ambassador to the congregation and to the world. To help a wide variety of people to unite as members of the body of Christ, and then to help them stay united in spite of each other's faults, was both challenge and delight. If one enjoys interaction and friendship with people and the feeling that one's life is useful, the pastor's life is ideal. Being a pastor is a recipe for great fulfillment. Service to and participation in the life of a local congregation has been a necessity, privilege, and pleasure throughout my adult life.

Biblical preaching is always a focal point for the pastor. Not all who attend church are mature believers. Furthermore, no matter how long we have been followers of Christ, we need to hear the gospel again and again. We need to be summoned regularly to trust, love, and serve God and God's people. Drifting out of vital discipleship happens. Evangelizing beyond the congregation is essential, but so is evangelizing in the congregation. God calls us to be a missionary people always seeking to be God's instruments in drawing others into the fellowship of faith in Christ. Preaching the gospel is always an awesome responsibility.

A pastor of a congregation has to be a generalist. The above descriptions of the pastor's duties and privileges make that clear. Pastor, preacher, worship leader, evangelist, teacher, friend, follower, leader, forgiver, community organizer, challenger—all the pastor's gifts and talents are on daily call.

Serving Beyond the Congregation—Within the ALC

The pastor of a congregation is necessarily involved in wider areas of the church's work. The congregations I served were members of the American Lutheran Church and of local councils of churches, and the pastor as well as laity represented the congregation in those settings. That meant a commitment to doing justice and working for unity in both church and the wider society. I had extraordinary opportunities to share in and represent the congregation's service beyond its borders.

Pastoral service in the life of the church beyond the congregation was especially extensive as I served as pastor of the University Lutheran Church of Hope in Minneapolis. While I did not know it at the time, my preparation for the ALC presidency was enhanced by service on a wide variety of ELC and ALC boards and committees during the twenty-three years as a parish pastor. For several years I chaired the ALC Board of Youth Activity. That board initiated and sustained many programs that assisted congregations in ministering to their youth. A national Luther League program for high school youth was supported and expanded. Youth leadership training led many young people to actual leadership positions in congregations and district and national levels of the ALC. Those leadership opportunities led the same youth to major leadership roles in the wider community as well. Every two years a national youth gathering sponsored by the Board of Youth Activity attracted 15,000 to 30,000 young people from ALC parishes. A week of worshipping, Bible studying, meeting in small groups, and listening to major national speakers was a winning experience for the young people. One especially high point was a spirited sermon by Dr. Martin Luther King Jr. during the beginning years of his civil rights leadership. Similar stirring testimonies came from such public luminaries as U.S. President Jimmy Carter, singer Pete Seeger, poet Maya Angelou, and Pastor Jesse Jackson. The week provided many moving moments in the lives of these thousands of young people. The Board of Youth Activity was also instrumental in obtaining and developing the remarkable Holden Village Retreat Center, a center that has enriched the lives of many in subsequent years. I also served as president of the ALC Bible Camp Association which included about twenty-five camps spread across the U.S. These camps are incredible resources as the country urbanizes and loses touch with God's creative majesty. Owned and operated by local clusters of congregations, the camps looked to the Board of Youth Activity for many services.

Numerous other opportunities for service to the church beyond the congregation were afforded me during my twenty-three years as parish pastor. I chaired the board of Bethesda Home for the Aged in South Dakota, was an early board member in a pioneering Plymouth Christian Youth Center in a difficult area of North Minneapolis, served as the ALC representative at a White House conference on equal opportunity, and served as a founding member of both national and Minnesota councils on religion and race. Serving on the Augsburg College Board of Regents was another rich experience.

Serving Beyond the Congregation—SEMPACC

In 1958, shortly after becoming pastor of the University Lutheran Church of Hope in Southeast Minneapolis, community organizing became a part of my job description. The pressing need for neighborhood renewal in the area in which the congregation was located made the action imperative. The community was threatened with urban blight. Hope congregation could not stand by and simply watch an urban disaster happen in its neighborhood. It was apparent that the congregation and its pastor had to carry their portion of responsibility for the wider community.

There was no city plan for the orderly development of Southeast Minneapolis. Its vibrant residential base was being overwhelmed by a series of incursions that threatened existing stable residential neighborhoods. The threats included:

1. A rapidly expanding spate of university student rooming houses with absentee landlords replacing family owners.

2. A rapidly increasing number of cheaply-constructed walk-up apartment buildings catering to a transient clientele.
3. An ancient city zoning map that had residential streets zoned for commercial and industrial use.
4. Diminishing school populations with threats of school closures.
5. An expanding university whose vast land needs often required home removal.
6. Freeways routed through prime Southeast Minneapolis residential areas causing removal of a large number of family residences.
7. A parking situation that was fast becoming unmanageable.
8. Business centers losing family-serving stores—banks, clothing stores, grocery stores, boutiques—to fast food outlets.
9. Loss of sense of community as all the above took their toll.

Southeast Minneapolis was on track to lose its neighborhood coherence and become an urban nightmare. At stake was the health of a significant segment of the city of Minneapolis. Furthermore, the University of Minnesota was in danger of being surrounded by an unmanageable, decaying landscape. To simply stand by and watch the neighborhood decay would have been a congregational denial of God's call to service.

The ten-member Southeast Minneapolis Clergy Association became convinced all segments of the community, congregations included, had to be rallied to meet the challenges. A large community organization was essential if anything was to happen that would stop the spreading urban blight. Cooperation from all segments of the Southeast Minneapolis community would be necessary to change course and stop the encroaching decay. Some of the pastors were in touch with other community organizations and knew that they also were looking for ways to pursue community health. A group of concerned Southeast Minneapolis persons, including representatives of the pastors, came together to form the Southeast Minneapolis Planning and Coordinating Committee (SEMPACC).

Our congregations were readily enlisted. They provided a variety of resources, including meeting rooms, volunteer personnel, modest sums of money, and a community-wide character. However, the congregations by themselves could not begin to challenge the prevailing neighborhood drift. The pastors, with Pastor Bob MacGregor of Andrew Presbyterian Church and I leading, made contact with other concerned individuals and groups. As word of a community-wide effort spread, it became apparent that there was a gold mine of residents and workers who shared concern for Southeast Minneapolis. Two vastly talented community homemakers, Norma Olson and Anne Barnum, gave endless hours and were organizing wizards. Two engineers, John Jamison and Joe Russell, began devoting large chunks of time to help create a broad-based community organization. A major industrial land developer, Fred Chute, offered his help. The Minneapolis City Planning Commission was contacted and provided an outstanding planner, Wei Ming Liu, to assist our neighborhood efforts. Contacts were made with three main neighborhood associations—Como, Marcy-Holmes, and Prospect Park. Business associations were approached. Of essential importance was the University of Minnesota. Key university leaders, beginning with the president, responded favorably to initiatives.

A SEMPACC governing board was formed that included representatives from the ministerial association, three neighborhood groups, three business associations, the University of Minnesota, and concerned individuals. Bob MacGregor, John Jamison, and I each served as chair during the early SEMPACC years. The genius of the organization, however, was the commitment of a core group of community volunteers. They were self-starters and produced extraordinary results.

It is important to note that my involvement in the wider community would not have been possible without the knowledge that I was acting on behalf of a congregation that had committed itself to participation in neighborhood and community renewal. SEMPACC simply became a part of my responsibilities as pastor of Hope Church. Through fourteen years of extensive community involvement, the congregation knew what I was doing and was consistently supportive. I believed my wider community work was a part of my pastoral calling.

In a very short time SEMPACC was active on several fronts. The work with City Planner Wei Ming Liu was of critical importance. There had to be a coherent plan for the Southeast Minneapolis community and that required heavy involvement from neighborhood representatives as well as the city planning staff. The zoning problems were an immediate threat, and SEMPACC representatives were a frequent presence at the city zoning office seeking changes in the zoning map. Density levels, parking requirements, and types of construction required consideration. Southeast schools were always on the front burner. Merging of the two Southeast high schools, Marshall High and University High, neither viable alone, was one of the early accomplishments. SEMPACC, the university, and the two schools hammered this out, and it was not easy. Transportation required regular attention. Street traffic patterns, truck routes, freeway noise abatement, public transit, and the endless parking problem all required neighborhood input. A group of SEMPACC members banded together and created a housing unit that purchased and resold homes in order to assure their single family character.

Relations with the University of Minnesota were crucial. Local residents feared the university would continually need more space at the expense of surrounding neighborhoods. Fortunately, the university president, regents, and staff recognized the stake the university had in maintaining healthy environs. They became full partners and assigned a key administration figure, Tommy Thompson, a vice president and personal assistant to the president, to be liaison to SEMPACC. Later the university engaged a staff person, Werner Shippee, to work full time on neighborhood concerns.

SEMPACC's increasing role in Southeast Minneapolis development was helped by two public officials who happened to be Southeast residents. Minneapolis Mayor Arthur Naftalin and State Representative Alpha Smaby were always ready to help. University presidents, particularly Malcolm Moos and Meredith Wilson, were always accessible and helpful in many ways. The merger of the two high schools would not have happened without university cooperation from the top.

All of this community work provided me with broad experience in Minneapolis public affairs. SEMPACC personnel became well known throughout the city. As a result, several of us were elected or appointed to public office. While those offices required new and broader responsibilities, they also positioned SEMPACC to pursue issues that affected Southeast as well as other Minneapolis neighborhoods. Bob MacGregor had been SEMPACC's point person on zoning matters. One of his chief motivations to run for city alderman was to be able to see that a new, up-to-date city-wide zoning ordinance was written. He was elected alderman, and one of his great accomplishments was helping to prepare and pass a new zoning ordinance. Because of her outstanding work in serving all segments of Southeast Minneapolis planning, Norma Olson was appointed to the City Planning Commission where she was a valued member for many years. John Jamison was SEMPACC's key person in transportation matters and, in a remarkable accomplishment, was appointed Minnesota State Highway Commissioner. Hal Holbrook was elected to the Minneapolis Park Board. I had been especially active in school matters; SEMPACC was able to be a strong supporter of quality public schools. When a vacancy occurred on the Minneapolis School Board, the remaining board members appointed me to fill the vacancy. In subsequent years I was twice elected to the school board in city-wide elections. While all of us continued our association with SEMPACC, other members had to take over the leadership roles.

There were many positive results from the SEMPACC efforts. I am writing this almost fifty years after we formed SEMPACC and can say confidently that SEMPACC's work has enabled Southeast Minneapolis to hold its own as a desirable living and working area. Accomplishments in which SEMPACC played an important role include the following:

1. Enactment of a new city-wide zoning ordinance. While many Minneapolitans were involved, the role of SEMPACC was crucial.

2. Three Southeast Minneapolis residential neighborhood associations became more knowledgeable and cooperative, with resultant success in maintaining strong residential neighborhoods.

3. Neighborhood elementary schools were sustained and improved. The high school could not be sustained, but specialized instruction and open enrollments in the high schools of contiguous areas of the city have done much to mitigate the loss. Southeast could have lost all its public schools without the organized strength that SEMPACC provided.

4. The University of Minnesota committed itself to partnering with the surrounding community in planning its geographical needs and solutions. For the first time it drew firm boundary lines, with a pledge not to move into adjacent residential areas.

5. Higher density private student housing was built in locations that did not threaten the residential neighborhoods. While threats of cheap, transient housing continue, the neighborhoods now know in advance of proposals and know how to use city powers in limiting them.

6. A new light rail line has been planned with community input, assuring that it will best serve and be least disruptive to the Southeast Minneapolis community.

7. Areas of Southeast Minneapolis zoned for industrial and commercial activity received community input on their new plans, and better uses have resulted.

8. Parking requirements for all new construction have been much improved and better enforced.

9. Community ambience is much improved. People work together on community projects, become acquainted with each other, and share broad concerns for community improvement.

Serving Beyond the Congregation—Minneapolis Board of Education

Appointment to the Minneapolis Board of Education in 1965 came as a result of extensive SEMPACC work for schools in the Southeast community. When the possibility of appointment appeared, it immediately raised the question of separation of church and state. It was taken for granted that appointment to fill a short, unexpired term meant a subsequent run for election. I knew there were many instances across the nation where pastors served as mayors, school board members, and in other public offices. Yet I also knew it was a touchy subject which could elicit strong differences of opinion. A number of things convinced me that such service was in order. A pastor, like all other members of the congregation, is a citizen of the state and ought to carry the same responsibility as others for the well-being of the state. The school board service was voluntary and unpaid and had historically been viewed as non-political. I was pleased to discover virtually no community antipathy about my service as a violation of separation of church and state, though I was often criticized for stances on other educational issues.

Deep grounding in public school affairs and awareness of the importance of public schools to both Southeast Minneapolis and the entire city convinced me that school board service would be a legitimate extension of the pastoral office. It was essential that the congregation would also see this as a legitimate part of my pastoral calling. The question was whether or not the public service of the congregation and I should extend beyond the Southeast Minneapolis community to include the entire city. After much discussion, the Hope Church council unanimously encouraged me. At no time then or subsequently was I aware of negative feelings from members of the congregation regarding my school board service. It was obvious the school board time would cut into family time, but my spouse and children encouraged me to accept the responsibility.

The school board was responsible for assuring quality education for 75,000 young people. The 1960s brought an avalanche of problems to the schools. Both educational and social problems were rife. To illustrate, the technological revolution raised a variety of questions that had to be addressed. Was the curriculum helping to prepare young people for productive life in a rapidly changing society? Many neighborhoods like Southeast were being threatened by urban developments. Economic disparity was causing rifts between schools both in more affluent and less affluent neighborhoods. Civil rights consciousness was inflamed, and the de facto segregated schools were among the chief areas of contention. It was a time when churches could not isolate themselves from the social unrest that had come especially to urban America.

By far the most difficult, tense, and challenging problem during my nine years on the school board was the desegregation of the Minneapolis schools. School issues were usually difficult and often contentious. Curriculum issues, class size, school lunches, busing, and athletic programs demanded attention. Deserving issues clamored for favored treatment, and anti-tax groups second guessed every spending decision. Setting the tax levy was always difficult. Resources were always limited. Personnel issues abounded. Negotiations with the Minneapolis Teachers' Union were difficult and often quite acrimonious. In 1967 the teachers went on strike for the first time in Minneapolis's history. Teacher pay was the central issue, and supporters on both sides of the issue were leaning on the school board as strongly as possible. Selecting a new superintendent for the first time in twenty-five years required special attention. Our selection, Dr. John B. Davis, proved to be one of the finest superintendents in the country.

The desegregation of the Minneapolis schools had one thing going for it. The board did not have to make the decision as to whether or not to desegregate. The 1954 U.S. Supreme Court decision required desegregation. How to do it was left to the local communities, with federal judges determining whether the actions proposed would effectively serve the purpose. Great numbers of Americans were not ready to accept the judgment of the court, however, and they prepared to do battle against desegregation of the schools.

Announcements that the school board was planning desegregation of the Minneapolis schools triggered a huge outpouring of anger from a sizable number of city citizens. It was obvious that desegregation would require a great deal of student transfer and busing. Neighborhood loyalties would be threatened. Racial hatred, so much a part of American life, would inevitably cause trouble. The issues were not only racial but also economic. African-American families were comparatively poor, and Caucasian-American children were comparatively affluent. Housing segregation had kept the two groups in separate schools. Now the children would have to overcome the realities of both racial and poverty prejudice, attend the same schools, and bring an end to centuries of racial segregation and educational inequality. Many parents who were accustomed to having educational privileges for their children fought any plan that required their children or their classmates to be bused. That desegregation was mandated by the federal government made no difference to many. The federal government was far away; the school board was local and provided a focus for venting anger and fighting desegregation.

The school board decided to make some relatively small changes while efforts to create a comprehensive city-wide plan were in process. The board proposed that two nearby elementary schools, one predominantly black and one predominantly white, would be paired and their students mixed in such way as to provide racial balance. School board members, the superintendent of schools, and other staff attended numerous neighborhood meetings in order to allay fears and win support. That the meetings were often heated is an understatement. After thorough preparation and considerable recrimination, the action was taken. While acceptance was slow, it did come and illustrated to the community that desegregating the schools could work.

I served as school board chair for two crucial years during the desegregation process. They were very busy years—challenging and sometimes frightening. In addition to maintaining a high level of parish service, I had to attend and often chair meetings called to give citizens a chance to express themselves on desegregation plans. There were meetings that threatened to become riots. Obscenities and personal threats were hurled at us. Even our children had to face threats. Phone calls and letters piled up both at church and at home. Most were bitterly anti-desegregation. One day Ann was at home with the children when two police officers came to the door. They told her the police had received an anonymous call saying a bomb had been placed in our home. They requested that Ann and the children leave, and then the police did a thorough search. No bomb was found, but we decided to play it safe and spent the night with relatives.

During these years I ran for re-election to the board. In an attempt to make a strong statement for the desegregation efforts, Harry Davis, a legendary Minneapolis African-American, and I ran as a team. On the one side we took a good deal of heat, and I had ample opportunity to experience the hatred of some Americans for African-Americans and those who publicly stood with them. The other, very satisfying side of it was that we were both elected by a landslide vote.

Harry Davis was a remarkable person. He grew up in a racially segregated neighborhood, contracted polio which left him with a life-long limp, and yet became a Golden Gloves boxing champion. For several decades he was the volunteer coach of Minneapolis Golden Glove teams that won national plaudits. He brought young African-Americans in from the streets to the gym and often back to school. He exemplified the American success story in working his way from entry level menial jobs to an executive position with the Minneapolis *Star Tribune* newspaper.

Harry and I were close friends as well as working partners. The same was true with Superintendent Davis and fellow board member, Stuart Rider. Those friendships have endured through the years and have been a rich part of my life.

Civil Rights Action

Racism has been a terrible blight throughout the history of the United States. Our country has had a difficult time making good on its bold assertion that "all men are created equal." Not even an incredibly brutal Civil War with its Emancipation Declaration could end the violent discrimination against the emancipated slaves and their descendants. By 1940 a significant shift in civil rights for all people was underway. The beginning integration of the U.S. armed forces was a decisive move. The 1954 Brown vs. Board of Education case requiring the opening of public schools to all Americans had huge implications. The Civil Rights Act of 1967 was the capstone of a quarter century of legal advance. The fact of racial segregation and discrimination was still very much the reality in spite of the gains. It became clear to me that God's call to "do justice" required action from congregations and their pastors.

My first personal exposure to the realities of segregated America began during my three-plus years in the U.S. Army during World War II, from 1943 to 1946. My army career included experiences that epitomized both the old and the emerging new era in civil rights. As a young acting corporal in World War II, I was assigned a week's duty in a segregated black battalion. All of the officers and non-commissioned officers were white. All of the "grunts" were black. The unit was a disaster. Fortunately for me a year later our officer's candidates class was commanded by an outstanding black candidate chosen by the white officers. The idea of inherent black inadequacy was made laughable. Later in my army life I served in a prisoner of war processing company whose personnel was half Japanese-Americans. Many of them had been sent to the notorious Japanese-American detention camps following Pearl Harbor. Now they had become essential personnel in a sensitive army unit. Many of them became my fast friends. The U.S. Army provided my first personal experiences of what the civil rights talk was all about.

It was not until returning to Minneapolis to be pastor of the University Lutheran Church of Hope that I found myself in the middle of the civil rights struggle. Congregational membership included two African-American and several Asian families. In addition the nearby University of Minnesota, many of whose students attended Hope Church, was deeply engaged in recruiting both students and faculty from minority communities. Pastoral concern for parishioners required that I be engaged with them in seeking racial justice and civil rights for all.

One of the decisive occasions for me was when a handsome young black couple began attending Hope Church. They asked for an opportunity to talk with me. From quick questioning while greeting worshippers at the front door I knew he was a heart doctor from the University of Pennsylvania doing graduate studies at the University of Minnesota. The couple told me an incredible story. For three months they had been living in a motel near Hope Church because they could not find an apartment to rent in Southeast Minneapolis or its environs. Whenever they found a vacant apartment they were told that the apartment "had just been rented" or "was no longer on the market." Here they were—a handsome young couple, the husband training to be a heart surgeon—and they were being refused housing because they were racially unacceptable.

Two things resulted. First, I helped the couple find an apartment in the area where most congregational members lived. Fortunately a good friend and member of Hope Church had just purchased a small apartment building in the Southeast Minneapolis community. I called him, told of the fine young couple's trouble, and asked if he could and would help. To my great relief and delight, he said there was a vacant apartment and the young couple could take occupancy immediately. I felt a significant victory had been won.

However, I was still left with the knowledge that Southeast Minneapolis neighborhoods were systematically excluding blacks from neighborhood housing. I had just read that the Minneapolis Council of Churches was seeking volunteers for a city-wide Fair Housing Committee. I responded and in short order was asked to chair the committee. I presented the possibility to the Hope Church council, informing them that I would be involved in attempts to break down the patterns of racial exclusion in the neighborhoods where most of our members lived. The council endorsed the proposal and encouraged me to be involved. The result was a series of neighborhood gatherings seeking to open Southeast Minneapolis housing to people regardless of race. Hope Church people opened their homes to invite their neighbors in to encourage open housing in their neighborhoods. Members of the congregation saw that justice required real changes in community acceptance of minority people.

It was clear to me that God's charge to do justice required the involvement of both congregation and staff of Hope Church in the civil rights struggle that was convulsing the country. Once started, I was a frequent speaker on civil rights at community and congregational events. My biggest contributions, however, were through the Minneapolis School Board and Minneapolis Urban Coalition. Supporting desegregation and racial justice was challenging, exciting, and harrowing.

One of the most moving experiences while school board chair was participation in the Maintenance Workers' March in Memphis, Tennessee. It followed the assassination of the Rev. Martin Luther King Jr., who had come to Memphis to march in support of the worker's battle for justice in wages and working conditions. The Memphis school janitors were also involved. Following King's death, the leaders of the planned march decided the march needed to go on, and they called for support. A group of downtown Minneapolis business leaders asked Minneapolis School Superintendent Davis and me to march. We did so, and it was a remarkable experience. To help commemorate King's planned participation, the march was entirely silent. Marchers assembled in an African-American neighborhood and marched through the downtown area and through largely white areas of the city. The mood of great sadness at King's death and the urgency of the civil rights cause he had come to support were palpable throughout the march. The silence was amazing. Thousands of marchers and tens of thousands of people lined the streets, and the only sound was the shuffling of feet and an occasional bird chirping. The downtown streets were jammed with people. National Guard members lined the streets to assure the march was peaceful. It had been announced that the National Guard was ordered out to protect the marchers. I was struck that they all, rifles at the ready, faced the marchers and not the onlookers who crowded sidewalks and from whom trouble was most likely to emanate.

It was such a passionate event. Martin Luther King Jr. having just "laid down his life for his friends" evoked incredibly deep feelings. There was a powerful awareness that this march was one of the capstones for the heart-rending, often violent civil rights struggle. Emotion simply filled the air. Ever since that Memphis march, I have felt that we participated in a turning point in the U. S. civil rights battle. The road to justice would still be long and hard, but comparatively speaking the road was now downhill.

Pastor Martin Luther King Jr. was a great inspiration for me. His prophetic-pastoral stance inspired multitudes of us. He addressed the nation and its governmental leaders in the biblical prophetic tradition. There was no mincing of words. Legislation was needed, enforcement of legislation was needed, and he called on the heads of government to provide the leadership in heeding the needs of the oppressed. He summoned all of us to step up and end the racism in our own lives and in the life of the total society. The words "freedom" and "justice" and "courage" rolled from his lips and reached across the nation. He did so while calling for non-violence and illustrating how that worked even in his own life.

Three times I had opportunity to be with Dr. King. The first time I served as his host when he addressed the ALC Youth Gathering in Miami. It was during my tenure as chair of the ALC Board of Youth Activity that we invited King to speak, in spite of his being at that time a very controversial figure. He captured our youth. At the next ALC national convention, Pastor David Brown, ALC youth executive, and I were required to explain and defend the board's invitation to King. We were glad for the opportunity.

The second time with Dr. King, I had been invited to be one of the founders of a U.S. Council on Religion and Race. About fifty of us from around the country formed the council. It was formed to let the world know that U.S. religious leadership was supporting the efforts for racial justice and peace led by Dr. King.

The third time was at the Capitol Mall in Washington, D.C. It was a moving moment to stand at the foot of the Washington Monument and see the solid mass of people absolutely filling the great mall all the way to the Lincoln Memorial. It was one of King's greatest days. His "I Have a Dream" speech has been heard by millions as it has been played again and again all over the world.

Urban Coalition

The 1960s civil rights era was a time of turmoil throughout the U.S. and especially in the inner cities of the country. The cities were hotbeds of demands, counter-demands, angry street gatherings, and marches. Minneapolis shared the experience with the whole country. I have alluded to the troubles in the city schools. The streets were even more threatening. Rioting, autos set on fire, looting, and acts of violence were the visible realities stemming from decades of racial prejudice and repression. Had it not been for the non-violent leadership of Martin Luther King Jr., the explosion of violence would have been much worse.

A Minneapolis Urban Coalition was formed to stem the violence in the streets and to provide positive responses to the just demands stemming from civil rights abuses. I was asked to be a member of it. Coalition members included the mayor, top leadership from the business and industrial sectors, educators, neighborhood leaders, and key leaders from the African-American community. Coalition efforts helped to end the rioting and provide means to address just grievances. Hope Church became one of the meeting places for the group. There were a great many meetings between representatives from minority and majority communities. Discriminatory practices, both short and long term, were addressed. Receiving immediate attention were such matters as discriminatory hiring practices, police profiling and abuse, delayed city services, and the strong sense of being left out of decision making in the public arena. The coalition provided a much needed alternative to the usual way of doing business through the bureaucratic maze of city government.

Meetings abounded on dozens of fronts. There was an abundance of anger and accusations and confrontation. The coalition provided the minority community access to the recognized movers and shakers of the city. It made a big difference when CEOs of General Mills, Pillsbury, and major downtown banks joined the mayor and city council members in making themselves personally available to minority representatives.

A description of one of the meetings that I was asked to attend was typical of the experiences of many coalition members. About fifteen fiery young leaders of the street protests asked me to meet them "on their turf," which was a settlement house in the heart of the African-American community. The concern was what they referred to as "dummy" classes and what the schools referred to as "remedial" classes. Because the preponderance of young students sent to these classes were African-Americans, it was assumed that they were discriminatory actions intended to demean black young people.

It was not a nice, orderly, sit-down meeting. The young men surrounded me, kept moving around while they denounced the school board for, in effect, declaring that black people are dumb. I kept insisting that the classes were inaugurated to help children who needed special help. I thought it was quite possible I would be physically attacked until I saw Josie Johnson, a legendary leader in the African-American community, sitting nearby. I knew then that, while a deeply felt grievance was being addressed, it was also political theater that was being played out around me.

The Urban Coalition was an important factor in restoring peace to the Minneapolis streets. In addition, it helped to start a chain of events that moved the city a long way toward racial equality and racial peace.

Minnesota has a large Native American population. Their civil rights plight was as desperate as those of African-Americans. In the post-World War II years, many Native Americans migrated from reservations to Minneapolis. The public schools were, of course, responsible for the education of their children. It was a challenging task. Many of the Native American children had very spotty educational backgrounds. Dropout rates were high. In order to meet their needs, small class size had to be maintained, school social workers made available, and special teacher training provided. The school district had to find assistance in funding the multiple needs of Native American students.

Chief among school board efforts to obtain funding assistance were requests to both the state and federal governments. We became lobbyists who called attention to the harsh injustices visited upon Native American people. Again, public schools were a major target for expressing anger and dissatisfaction. Drop-out rates were staggering, and graduation rates depressing. Funding was an immediate problem. School board members along with the superintendent presented the needs before both state and national legislative bodies.

One of the most harrowing and satisfying days occurred when Superintendent Davis and I traveled to Washington, D.C., for appointments with congressional members and with U.S. Vice President Hubert Humphrey. We were supporting national efforts for increased funding to meet the special needs of Native American students. After meeting with members of Congress, we had a few hours free time before a late afternoon meeting with Vice President Humphrey.

Though we had read that civil rights protests were to be held that day, we decided to visit Resurrection City, a large assemblage of tents and shacks that housed hundreds of people on the Capitol Mall. The residents were mostly poor and mostly minorities, and they spent their time lobbying and demonstrating at the Capitol and elsewhere. As we left Resurrection City, a violent fight broke out between two groups of young men, one white and one black. One young man grabbed a baseball bat and knocked out one of his opponents with a blow to the head. Several others were knocked to the ground. The melee broke up as police sirens were heard. I thought surely there must have been deaths. However, I looked in the next day's papers and the brawl was not even mentioned. At the least there must have been lasting injuries.

As we arrived at the Foggy Bottom old State Department building where Vice President Humphrey had his office, an ancient school bus pulled up at the front entrance. Mexican-Americans began pouring out of the bus, obviously to make some sort of protest. Policemen who were protecting the building and its personnel waded into the protesters with their night sticks flailing. Again we heard the sickening sound of clubs hitting heads. However, the police action was much less severe, and all the protesters managed to get back on the bus and leave.

The meeting with Vice President Humphrey was the satisfying part of the day. Both Superintendent Davis and I had known Humphrey during his days as Minneapolis mayor and then as Minnesota senator. Hence the meeting had something of an "old home" occasion. We had a lengthy discussion about civil rights issues and especially about the educational needs for Native American young people. The Vice President responded positively to our expressions regarding financial support from federal sources. He assured us he would take up the cause, and subsequently the Minneapolis schools received significant aid through the Bureau of Indian Affairs.

A Lesson from Parish Years

Awareness of the importance of the local congregation was constantly reinforced during my years as parish pastor. The vision of God's work in the world kept expanding in scope and excitement. The conjunction of individual faith and piety with unity in the body of Christ and global ministry for justice and peace expanded my horizons. Already as parish pastor I felt myself engaged as a Christian pastor in the global Christian church and in the global society.

CHAPTER THREE

President/Presiding Bishop

Introduction

My election to high national office in the American Lutheran Church was totally unexpected. In 1968 I was serving as pastor of the University Lutheran Church of Hope when several colleagues who had worked closely with me nominated me for the vice presidency of the ALC. It came as a surprise, because nobody had talked to me about it until a couple of days before the electing convention. The nomination came, I believe, because a rapidly changing society was requiring a greater congregational and pastoral involvement in wider circles than the congregation alone. Other congregations and pastors were making the same discovery, and something of a groundswell developed. I was noticeable because Minneapolis was the urban hub for an area that included a major part of the ALC constituency. Even so, being elected vice president was more surprising than the nomination had been.

The possibility that I might become the president of the ALC did not occur to me until I was elected vice president. It was already known that a 1970 retirement of President Fred Schiotz would require the election of a new president of the ALC, hence I had to think about the possibility of being nominated for that office. While it was unusual to move directly from the parish to the church presidency, I believed the two positions required the same gifts and so I determined to accept the nomination. I thought the president should be first and foremost the chief pastor of the ALC and that service as parish pastor both in small town and large city provided excellent preparation. The two years of service on the ALC Church Council as vice president brought me up to date on the policies and ministries of the ALC.

However, the ALC convention in August 1970 seemed to end the possibility that I would serve as president. Dr. Kent Knutson, president of Wartburg Seminary, my seminary classmate, former parishioner, and good friend, was elected president, and I was re-elected vice president. A previous convention had voted to restructure the operational style of the ALC. In addition to all the other responsibilities of the president, Kent had the responsibility to oversee the actual implementation of the restructuring plan.

At the October 1972 ALC convention Kent reported on the near completion of the restructuring and on the church's work in many other areas. I was on the rostrum with Kent throughout the convention and had no inkling that he was ill. A week after the convention's close Mrs. Knutson called to tell me that Kent had not felt well during the convention and was now very ill and had been hospitalized. She did not think it wise for him to receive visitors at that time, but suggested I be ready to take on added responsibilities. A couple of days later I was able to visit Kent and was shocked to find him unable to talk intelligibly, although he clearly understood and was able to sit up in bed for an embrace. Kent's illness progressed rapidly, and by the end of December he was unconscious and had been diagnosed as a victim of Jacob Kreuzfeldt's Disease. It was announced that there was no known cure.

I began serving as acting ALC president on January 1, 1973. It was a difficult time. We still prayed that a miraculous healing would occur. However, Kent died in March, and I was installed as president shortly thereafter. I served the remaining years of the term and in the ensuing years was elected twice to six-year terms. In 1986 I was elected president for the remaining year before the formation of the Evangelical Lutheran Church in America (ELCA) on January 1, 1988.

The following pages are my attempt to make a coherent, brief estimate of ALC missions and ministries from 1973 to 1987, with heavy emphasis on those areas where I was most strongly involved. I find it helpful to describe the work of the ALC in four sections: service *to* congregations, service *on behalf of* congregations, ecumenical expressions, and the church in the public square. These sections correlate closely with the four priorities described earlier in this paper: evangelism, congregations, unity, and justice. Obviously there is a great deal of overlap. Evangelism, for instance, is involved in all four priorities simultaneously.

Pastoral Character of Work as President

Christian congregations join in creating national church bodies and councils for three main reasons: to express the unity of the church of

Christ, to provide services to the congregations, and to exercise shared faith through missionary efforts and humanitarian service both locally and throughout the world.

A church leader, whether serving in a local parish or in a national church body, is first and foremost a pastoral leader and is considered as such by the church constituency. It was for that reason that I felt comfortable moving from the parish directly into the ALC presidency. To trust in and to spread the gospel—the good news of God's love through the life, work, suffering, death, and resurrection of Jesus—is the chief work of Christian believers. The natural corollary to that is for believers to serve the public good, to express love for one's neighbors throughout the world by "doing justice, loving kindness, and walking humbly with God" (Micah 6:8). Those tasks were always before me as a parish pastor, and they continued as I served as the pastor president of the American Lutheran Church.

There is great congruity in the work of a congregational pastor and a church body president. A pastor or bishop must be a generalist, one called to leadership roles on many fronts. Both pastor and bishop are preachers, teachers, worship leaders, witnesses, unifiers, listeners, counselors, community leaders, and friends. In both roles I found the work interesting, often exciting, occasionally frustrating, and, I hope and believe, useful. Overall I believe the ALC accomplishments were substantial and significant during my years in office.

Administration

Parish experience was of great help in preparing me for the administrative tasks required of the ALC president. The congregations I served had a small number of staff persons, but providing leadership for a small staff requires many of the same skills that are required when working with a large staff. Working with lay leadership, meeting with church councils, planning and coordinating services essential to congregational life and health, all require the same capabilities necessary for leadership in a large church body. I felt well prepared to become administrative officer of the ALC.

The two primary decision-making bodies in the ALC were the biennial General Convention and the ALC Church Council. The thousand-delegate convention was the ultimate authority in the ALC. Delegates were direct representatives of the congregations, elected at the district conventions. The forty-person Church Council was elected by the ALC General Convention to handle church affairs between conventions and to prepare agendas for the next convention. In order to assure the congregational character of the church and the crucial role of lay leadership, four rules governed selection of delegates. One, the number of pastoral delegates was limited. Two, persons employed by the ALC could not be elected delegates. Three, bishops were given the right to speak but could not serve as delegates. Four, the council elected its own chair who was traditionally a lay person. Elected chair during my years were Lloyd Jacobson from Minnesota, Bruce Howe from North Dakota, Addison Dewey from Ohio, Don Hall from Washington, and H.W. Pfennig from Texas. Each provided superior service and were my close personal friends

The biennial conventions of the church were wonderful occasions. The worship services and Bible studies were inspiring. The hymn singing was stirring. The one thousand delegates from the congregations of the ALC heard program unit leaders describe their work, their problems, their opportunities, and their needs. After open hearings, questions, and debate, the convention would adopt plans and budget for the ensuing two years.

Presiding at conventions was a very important duty for the president. The thousand delegates were there to do the business of the church of Christ. They wanted to know about the world-wide extended ministries their congregations had helped to establish and support. They wanted opportunities to question, debate, and be heard on the critical issues facing the church. They expected to be involved in determining the future course of the ALC. Convention business had to be grounded in the Christian faith, done fairly, clearly, crisply, and with good humor. The well-being of the national programs of the church depended on the congregations' enthusiasm for and loyalty to the church's program. On returning home the delegates would be reporting to their own congregations and to clusters of nearby congregations. I believe ALC delegates returned home from every convention enthused about the ministries of the ALC. Their personal reports were of great help in maintaining the constituency's confidence in their church's program and staff.

The American Lutheran Church's constitution provided for a collegial administration of the ALC national offices. Each unit had a board or a committee that gave congregations direct participation in the planning and work of the national offices. The president partnered with those boards and committees in searching for and calling unit directors and in determining each unit's plan for action. Unit heads were given maximum freedom and responsibility. It was the president's responsibility to see that staff members worshipped together, worked together, cooperated with each other as a matter of course, and performed their duties with skill and spirit. The president's cabinet included the chief officer for each of the various divisions and offices. Regular meetings enabled cabinet members to envision the whole picture of the church at work, cooperate closely, avoid duplication, encourage each other, and rejoice in each other's successes.

I was very proud of the caliber of persons attracted to leadership positions in the ALC national offices. The ALC was more than ably served by the three vice presidents elected to serve with me: first Bishop Gordon Huffman, then President Fred Meuser of Trinity Seminary, and then President Lloyd Svendsbye of Luther Seminary. After providing outstanding service in the president's office, two of my chief aides proved their mettle by being elected presidents of ALC institutions. Robert Vogel became a brilliant president of Wartburg College. Roger Fjeld became president of Wartburg Seminary and did superior work in that position. Morris Sorenson came from heading the world mission unit and, following outstanding service in my office, moved to a similar position in the ELCA. Robert Hoyt and Edward Schneider also served with distinction in the president's office. Arnold Mickelson's leadership as ALC General Secretary was of such quality that he was subsequently asked to be executive secretary for the Commission on a New Lutheran Church (CNLC). His successor was Kathryn Baerwald, a practicing attorney who came from a law firm to be the ALC General Secretary. Albert Anderson was the ALC's very successful manager of Augsburg Publishing House, the publishing arm of the church. Anderson also served the church in many other leadership posts. Morris Sorenson, Mark Thomsen, and Lowell Hesterman were long-time foreign missionaries who provided excellent leadership for the Division for World Mission and Interchurch Cooperation (DWMIC). The Division for Service and Mission in America (DSMA) executive, James Bergquist, had been dean at Trinity Seminary and prior to that was a staff person in the World Council of Churches (WCC). Paul Hanson came directly from being the much-loved pastor of a large congregation to head the Division for Life and Mission in the Congregation (DLMC). Executive directors of ALC Women were exceptional people—Alida Storaasli, Margaret Wold, and Bonnie Jensen.

Walter Wietzke, executive for the Division for Theological Education and Ministry (DTEM), was in office on my arrival and provided consistent, superior leadership. Norm Fintel left his position as director for the Division for College and University Services (DCUS) to become president of Roanoke College. Loren Anderson, who came from a vice presidency at Concordia College to head DCUS, went on to provide sterling leadership as president of Pacific Lutheran University. Glenn Nelson was an outstanding professor and academic dean at Luther College before succeeding Anderson as director of DCUS. Ron Matthias, Wartburg College professor, was Nelson's very capable successor. John Bachman came from the Wartburg College presidency to be an exceptionally capable director for the Office of Communication and Mission Support (OCMS), On retirement he was succeeded by Roald Kindem, an eminent parish pastor, and then by Herb David, an accomplished journalist. David Rokke served as assistant to George Schulz, executive for the Board of Trustees, and became Schulz's successor. Ed Bersagel was assistant to the South Dakota bishop before directing the Office of Support to Ministries (OSM). Charles Lutz brought a broad background in social ministry to head the Office of Church and Society (OCS). Fritz Treptow headed the Board of Pensions with distinction. John Houck was DSMA director on my arrival, but left shortly to become executive secretary of the Lutheran Council USA. It was always important for me to be friends with work colleagues. I was consistently blessed by deep friendships throughout the ALC and especially with members of the ALC administrative cabinet. Such friendships greatly enriched my life, and I believe those friendships contributed to the good spirit of the entire ALC.

One of my first tasks was to complete the implementation of a church-wide ALC restructuring and to make sure the new offices were functioning effectively. President Knutson had done the heavy lifting, but I was responsible for finishing the work. It proved fortuitous, for it enabled immediate involvement with boards and staff of every unit in planning and fulfilling program goals. The descriptive restructuring title was "Toward Greater Effectiveness in Mission." I believe the ALC fulfilled that mandate during my fifteen years in office.

Working Principles

Several working principles provided focus for my work as ALC president. A reading of my articles in the *Lutheran Standard*, *Acts*, and *The Month That Was* (a presidential review of the month's activity that was shared with ALC leadership) and my district and national convention speeches indicates how much these principles informed my thinking and acting. They were:

1. That the president shall uphold and take inspiration from the Scriptures, the Lutheran Confessions, and the constitution of the ALC .

2. That the president should be first and foremost a pastor called to witness to the Triune God in as many ways as possible.

3. That the ALC should maintain the primacy of missionary witness to the gospel of Jesus Christ.

4. That the ALC must be a vigorous supporter of the world's poor by both direct service aid and by public advocacy for justice, freedom, and peace for all people in all places. This must be understood as a necessary complement to and never an alternative to the missionary command.

5. That ALC national offices are to provide services that help equip the saints for mission in the local congregations and throughout the world.

6. That the ALC should be pro-active in expressing unity in Christ with both Lutheran and non-Lutheran Christians.

7. That reporting to the ALC constituency on national and international work with frequency and transparency should be a hallmark of the presidency and the national offices.

8. That esprit is essential for a church body and should be worked at and earned by individual believers, local congregations, and national offices.

Esprit

Since high school and college days I have been aware of the necessity of esprit in any group activity. I was an avid athlete, and early on it became apparent that while talent was important it was often esprit that decided the outcome. Inspirational leadership, teamwork, enthusiasm, excitement, mutual encouragement, staying power, the sense that challenges could be met and overcome, are ingredients of a team that plays with high esprit.

My three plus years in the U.S. Army made me even more aware of the essential character of high esprit. I served in units where morale was low and in units where morale was high. There was enormous difference in the performance of such units. It was obvious that the difference was due not to superior talent but to group esprit.

I brought that experience into my life as a pastor and church leader. From my first days as president of the ALC I believed esprit was an absolute necessity in a church body and its component parts. The church always needs to be a spirited, united, grace-filled, enthusiastic band of disciples seeking to bear witness to the power and love of God with both word and deed. Esprit is difficult to define, but morale flags without it. People know when it is present. One can only generalize about the spirit of a large group of people. Esprit in the ALC was high all the years I served as a parish pastor, and I believe that esprit was sustained and strengthened during my years as president. The bulk of ALC believers were enthusiastic about doing the mission of the church. They were enthusiastic about the ALC's foreign mission emphasis and its strong efforts to start new congregations in the U.S. There was deep affection for and loyalty to the church's seminaries and colleges. Support for the world's poor was manifested in many ways. There was appreciation for and trust in the various national staff persons who sought to assist in "equipping the saints." There was confidence in the pastors, missionaries, and other personnel who represented the church all over the world. There was an enthusiastic and responsible ecumenical spirit. There was readiness to be engaged in the public square. There was a sense that the ALC was "on the move." Esprit was present, and morale was good.

One of my duties was to be a "cheerleader" for the work of the church. A church's president has unique opportunity to see the many ways in which the church serves God and humanity, and those realities need to be known by the constituency. Written descriptions are essential, but personal sharing is the most effective. I preached in congregations frequently and reported to innumerable ALC conventions and gatherings. I used these many opportunities to tell ALC people about the far-flung missions and services they were supporting. I believed it necessary for church members to share the excitement of their missionary outreach and life-giving aid. It also helped to strengthen the unity of the global church of Christ, for so much of the work was done cooperatively with other churches.

The entire national church staff cadre built esprit through their service. A collegial working style was basic. Together we made certain that we were indeed engaged in the Lord's work. There was confidence that our work was useful and productive and that it was being received with gratitude. There was appreciation for each other and awareness that the entire staff was functioning as a team. The same was true with respect to the district bishops and staffs. The meetings of national office cabinet and council of bishops were overwhelmingly positive. We believed in what we were doing together, we cheered for each other, and the result was great enthusiasm and excitement. Differences of opinion were freely aired without recrimination. That was especially important as we proceeded toward merger, for the differences of opinion were strong. It would have been easy to develop contentious and downbeat attitudes.

The matter of esprit was especially important during the 1970s and 1980s. Christian individuals and congregations had to both affirm and strengthen their faith in the gospel while seeking ways to provide leadership and service in a rapidly changing society. Most mainline Protestant churches were having a difficult time during those years. Membership was falling, in-fighting was severe, youth were disappearing from the churches, and diminishing finances were causing serious cutbacks in mission services. Anti-institutionalism was in full flower. Large organizations were suspect, including government, corporations, universities, and national church bodies. What was purported to be a freer, simpler life was being touted. Protest movements flourished, old clothes became symbols of a new freedom, and conventional lives with conventional morals were shunned. For many youth and adults "church" was seen as a cultural hand-me-down that needed to be abandoned. The ALC could easily have suffered as much as some other churches, but it did not. Instead, the ALC was able to stay on course and maintain the loyalty and enthusiasm of its members. It was, I believe, a matter of esprit!

CHAPTER FOUR

NATIONAL OFFICES SERVING CONGREGATIONS

As previously indicated, I considered the national programs of the church to be work initiated by and supported by the congregations. The offices and programs briefly described in the following pages are, in effect, the congregations at work.

Services for Congregations

Division for Life and Mission in the Congregation (DLMC)

Parish Education

The ALC Division for Life and Mission in the Congregation provided a wide variety of services to assist congregations in being lively centers of mission. After twenty-three years as an ALC parish pastor, I had some strong opinions about one of the most important DLMC services (i.e., materials for parish education). My experience was that ALC parish education materials had been too difficult for both parish volunteer church school teachers and children. The confirmation materials were also too advanced and complicated for young people and their teachers. After becoming president I discovered that only fifteen percent of ALC congregations were using ALC parish educational materials. Shortly thereafter I recommended that Pastor Paul Hanson be called as the director of the ALC Division for Life and Mission in the Congregation (DLMC). I knew Paul well from seminary days and from close contact through his many years of outstanding work in parish ministry, including in the educational field, and was aware of his hard-driving, collegial, and compassionate spirit. During our years as parish pastors we had talked at length about the need for new educational materials in ALC congregations.

Similar conversations were held with Al Anderson, manager of the ALC's Augsburg Publishing House. His frustration level was high because of the poor sales and the small amount of publishing of ALC parish education materials being done by Augsburg Publishing House. I knew Al, too, as a brilliant and devoted churchman who sought to provide the best possible materials for ALC congregational use.

Shortly after Paul's arrival, I arranged a meeting in my office with Paul and Al. It was the first of several fruitful meetings. We shared the same sense of urgency for a new start at parish education materials. It quickly became apparent that there would be no turf battles between the DLMC and Augsburg Publishing House, a matter that had previously been troublesome. Before that first meeting was over it was agreed that the two units would be full partners in developing new materials. It was also determined that the materials would be intensely biblical, reflective of a Lutheran understanding of the faith, simple to teach, colorful, and reasonably priced.

The two units immediately established several joint working teams, including staff from both units for parish education, evangelism, worship, stewardship, and parish administration. The parish education group created a new series of Sunday school and vacation Bible school materials in record time. The congregational reception was heartening. Confirmation materials followed a similar path, as did Bible study material for adult education. Staff was provided for conducting teacher workshops all over the country. Within a year it was a new day for congregational use of ALC parish education materials.

At the completion of the fifteen years of my tenure, the use of ALC materials by ALC congregations had just reversed. Now eighty-five percent of congregations used ALC materials and were enthusiastic about their use. In addition there were strong sales to other church bodies and even to the U.S. military. Most important was that national staff persons, servants of the congregations, were providing Christian materials that helped young people to be strengthened in Christian faith and witness. Young people, even those from strong Christian homes, need to be evangelized. Parish education is always a prime source of gospel outreach.

In addition to its work in parish education the DLMC assisted congregations in many other ways. Adult Bible studies, worship materials, youth activities, and work with ALC Women (ALCW) required congregational training programs, liaison, and many other staff tasks. I was especially involved in the planning for work with youth and women, often meeting with their officers and frequently speaking at rallies and conventions.

Youth Activities

Churches always find it a challenge to pass the faith to the next generation. National church youth programs were being jettisoned by many Protestant churches in the 1960s and 1970s. Many church leaders had concluded that organized church youth work was no longer useful in the face of an often rebellious and critical youth. That spirit infected the ALC to some degree. In the previously mentioned church-wide restructuring, the previous Board of Youth Activity was eliminated. Responsibilities for youth work were transferred to DLMC with a considerable drop in financial support.

DLMC leaders and I had been engaged in youth ministry for many years and did not accept the conventional wisdom that organized church work with youth was passé. The ALC maintained a strong focus on youth ministries through its educational programs, work camps, local, regional, and national Luther League groups, church colleges, and campus ministries. Regional leadership training programs were very effective. National and regional youth gatherings attracted and challenged tens of thousands of young people and gave the youth opportunity to meet with outstanding leaders in church and society. Many young people participated in short term mission and work projects. In addition the ALC intentionally encouraged independent Lutheran groups who established various excellent youth ministries.

It was not always easy, but I believe the ALC's youth work helped large numbers of the church's youth to keep the faith, pursue discipleship, provide a leadership cadre for the church, and make a strong contribution to the overall life and work of the church.

Women in the Church

The ALC Women's organization (ALCW) was a powerful leadership and serving group in the life of the ALC. As parish pastor I had discovered the great strength in faith and works of congregational women's groups. They prayed together, studied the Bible, enjoyed each other, took care of each other, provided substantial financial support for the church, and were always ready to take on discipleship duties. The women's national organization was of the same spirit. The support of the ALC Women was of great help to the church at large and to me personally.

Women have always been at the heart of the church's life. In spite of obvious male dominance in leadership positions in the past, women provided more than their share of the muscle and sinew of the church. Discipleship involves devotion to God, congregational and wider fellowship, life-long learning in the Scriptures, prayer, ministries of mercy, and the pursuit of justice for all. Women have been leaders in such essential elements of Christian life.

As a parish pastor I became keenly aware that if help was needed for any good cause the pastor would be wise to start by asking the women to help. They exercised indispensable leadership even when the men held the offices. The same was true in our national programs. The organized women of the church were always at the cutting edge of the work of the church. I knew they could be called upon in any exigency. ALCW presidents Margaret Bauman, Fern Gudmestad, Elaine Donaldson, and Marlene Engstrom provided outstanding leadership.

Further, other moves toward full participation of women advanced during my years in office. Women's ordination to pastoral ministry coincided with my arrival in national office. The number of women pastors increased dramatically in a short period of years. Similarly, women serving on the national staff and on major boards of the church became commonplace. Kay Baerwald, a lay person and attorney, was the first woman to be elected ALC General Secretary, one of the three elected general officers. In congregations and in church institutions women assumed leadership positions. The ALC was greatly strengthened by their leadership.

Division for College and University Services (DCUS)

ALC church colleges have always been viewed as essential in educating leadership for the church. Fourteen outstanding ALC colleges were founded and developed by the immigrant Lutherans who were the pioneers of the ALC. All American church colleges have faced the temptation to drop their Christian commitment and concentrate completely on secular educational excellence. The ALC colleges have continued to be institutions seeking to be centers of both faith and learning. I called the ALC colleges the "jewels" of the church. They have been invaluable in helping provide both church and society with excellent and principled leadership. Their struggle to keep the Christian faith central to human life puts them in the front lines of the church's effort to maintain faith in Christ as the organizing center for a life of Christian vocation. It is exciting to see outstanding faculties helping young people to prepare for leading roles in both church and society.

College presidents and boards are central to that effort. I participated in the process each time college regents were called upon to engage a new college president. In every instance the new presidents proved to be outstanding educational leaders and led faculties in the struggle to understand and implement the colleges' commitment to the Christian faith and church. I take great pride in the achievements of ALC colleges. It has been a privilege to support and encourage them.

Division executives were outstanding. Norman Fintel, Loren Anderson, and Ron Matthias were wise counselors to and passionate supporters of the colleges. Fintel and Anderson moved on to became presidents of colleges of the church, and Matthias served another of the colleges as chief financial officer.

Division for Theological Education and Mission (DTEM)

A well-trained clergy thoroughly grounded in the Bible and the Lutheran Confessions, called to be preachers of the gospel and with personal commitment to Christ and church, was a hallmark of ALC parish life. ALC congregations created seminaries in order to assure a cadre of well-trained clergy. The national church offices were always deeply involved in the life of the seminaries. All the units of the church had a big stake in the seminaries, for seminary-trained pastors would become key persons in implementing the church's commitment to evangelical outreach and faithful service. The seminary graduates would be especially important in both the use of and evaluation of national office programs.

As president I looked to the seminary faculty for leadership in many elements of the church's life beyond the seminaries. They provided outstanding theological scholarship and inspirational leadership through their teaching and preaching outside as well as inside the seminary walls. Whenever a theological problem faced the church, the seminary faculties were called on to assure the best possible consideration of the issues. I visited the three seminaries frequently and spoke with faculty and students about the church and its expectations and hopes for a learned and inspiring cadre of clergy. I chaired the meetings at which the seminary presidents were elected. Of special significance during my years was a very successful church-wide Seminary Appeal that provided over thirty million dollars for the three ALC seminaries at a time when financial support was crucial. American Lutheran Church seminaries were solid contributors to the health and well-being of the church. Their commitments to God, the gospel, and the Lutheran Confessions were crucial in giving direction to the whole church.

A highlight during my years was the establishment of several regional centers for the continuing education of pastors. The outstanding DTEM director, Walter Wietzke, was untiring in his efforts to establish and undergird these centers. Ongoing course work was offered by theological faculties. Because of these regional centers, pastors from a local area were able to study together and share experiences and insights without lengthy absences from their parishes. It was another important way by which the national offices could serve ALC congregations. I believed these centers to be very important and assisted in obtaining funding for them.

Board of Trustees

The Board of Trustees, while much of its work seemed institutional in character, provided essential services for the congregations. Planning and recommending church-wide ALC budgets after consultation with all the units of the church was a huge and necessary task. It was essential that I be deeply engaged in that process. I met with staffs and boards of the many units and helped shape their requests for funds. Then I met with the trustees in making final determinations of budget priorities.

The productive investment of large sums of money was a very important work of the trustees. Pension funds alone ran into the hundreds of millions of dollars. Pastors and other personnel depended on those funds. Mission funds from ALC congregations often came in a flood one part of the year and were skimpy in another. As a result short-term investing and borrowing became very important.

The ALC had the volunteer services of outstanding professional investment persons. I regularly met with trustees and investment personnel so that I could assure the ALC constituency of complete integrity, capability, and transparency in the handling of the church's financial resources. The fact that the trustees consistently provided investment results that exceeded standard expectations was a great plus for the church. Trust in the responsible stewardship of funds is an absolute necessity in any organization, but especially in the life of churches. Both George Schultz and David Rokke, the trustees' executives during my years, earned and received that trust.

Services on Behalf of Congregations

Mission outreach was at the heart of the life of the national offices of the American Lutheran Church. All of the church offices knew they were a part of the extended missionary effort of ALC congregations, but they also knew two units, DWMIC and DSMA, were particularly responsible.

Division for World Mission and Interchurch Cooperation (DWMIC)

DGM was responsible for ALC missionary work beyond U.S. borders. Three things in the world mission area in which I was deeply involved deserve special mention. First, contrary to many other church bodies, the ALC continued seeking and sending out persons who were committed to long-term overseas missionary witness. Second, there was recognition of the growth of indigenous church bodies that carried their own responsibility for missionary outreach. In those instances the ALC "partnered" with the churches and made sure the ALC was the "junior" partner. Third, the ALC continued to show its missionary priority by providing the necessary funds to maintain a vigorous world missionary effort. A Global Mission Appeal planned and completed while I was in office provided over forty million dollars of new funding. Annual budgetary allocations evidenced the ALC's high priority for world missions.

In my frequent Sunday preaching to congregations I told congregants of the great and important work their missionaries were doing. The same was true at the annual district conventions at which I spoke. I visited missionaries whenever possible and let them know of the ALC's ongoing commitment to their work. I spent quality time with ALC missionaries and indigenous pastors in Tanzania, Ethiopia, Papua New Guinea, South Africa, Namibia, Hong Kong, Taiwan, Japan, and Mexico. There were more requests for visits to ALC missionaries and to the indigenous churches than I could meet. When unable to meet requests for such visits, I made a practice of asking ALC district bishops to go in my stead, confident they would use those opportunities to generate mission support among their constituencies.

The ALC Division for World Mission and Interchurch Cooperation maintained close liaison and supportive working relationships with several independent mission societies. A number of ALC pastors served as missionaries with the World Mission Prayer League, the Santal Mission, and Wycliffe Bible Translators. In many parts of the world ALC missionary personnel partnered with Lutheran missionaries from other countries. In other missionary areas they maintained close working relationships with other Protestant and often Roman Catholic and Orthodox personnel as well

Division for Service and Mission in America (DSMA)

New Congregations

Missionary outreach inside the U.S. was focused especially on the starting of new congregations. A majority of existing ALC congregations were in rural and small town America. It was a time of rapid population shift from rural into urban areas. Starting new congregations in urban areas required a great deal of "up front" personnel and money. Populations had to be surveyed to see if there were people who would help start a congregation. Property had to be purchased, usually at prices far exceeding what had been the case in smaller cities and rural areas. Advance funding was needed to get a first unit built. Pastors had to be called and supported before there was a congregation to support them. Advance planning and preparation were crucial. Through the DSMA the congregations of the ALC provided such early financing, planning, and preparation for new congregations.

Approximately thirty new congregations were started annually. In 1984, with staff initiative and my encouragement, a "50 More in '84" program was successfully completed. In that year the ALC started fifty new congregations in addition to the usual thirty. While the ALC could not meet all the mission opportunities, a large number of lively new congregations came into being. Some moved to self-support very rapidly, others more slowly. Many new congregations in impoverished and ethnic minority areas required long-term financial support. I made a point of visiting and encouraging as many of these as possible. I had exciting times with an Hispanic congregation in Surprise, Arizona; a Chinese congregation in Seattle, Washington; a Caribbean congregation in Brooklyn, New York; a Haitian congregation in Homestead, Florida; and predominantly African-American congregations in several cities.

All of us involved in the ALC's mission outreach efforts were aware of how much more could have been done with additional resources. At the same time we were inspired by the people in those new congregations and were thankful for and encouraged by how much was accomplished.

Social Services

In the major restructuring plan cited, the DSMA became responsible for ALC social services. The intent was to indicate that mission outreach and social service were inextricably linked. U.S. Lutheran people have always been active in doing works of love that are commonly called social services. Early immigrant congregations used their collective strength to found and support hundreds of nursing homes, orphanages, hospitals, and other forms of social services that were needed in American communities. Great changes have taken place in subsequent years, but those social services continue to be essential elements in the church's mission. Most of the church-owned nursing homes continue to exist though in different forms. A few of them remain under direct church ownership, but most are owned by independent Lutheran groups. The Evangelical Lutheran Good Samaritan Society for instance, started by a single ALC pastor and congregation, now has about 240 such facilities for senior citizens. The orphanages have been superseded by adoption agencies, group homes, and foster homes. Many such agencies are now operated by Lutheran Social Services (LSS), a joint Lutheran effort organized in fourteen regional bodies. LSS has a variety of other social service programs designed to help people in difficult straits. DSMA became responsible for liaison with these various groups, often serving as the accrediting agency for them. On the hospital front, there are a number of hospitals that are still owned by groups of Lutheran congregations, but practically speaking they operate independently. The need for public governance of hospitals has become increasingly evident, and the church's role has correspondingly diminished. The church's initial and sustaining role in social services has been invaluable.

Para-Church Activity

It is a temptation for church bodies to insist on bringing all church work under the governance of the national church body. However, the ALC had a history of affirming and assisting para-church service organizations. I strongly encouraged such work because it had worked in the ALC, required strong local initiative, and was an excellent counter to the strong public antipathy toward larger bureaucratic organizations. Illustrations of such activity were Lutheran Youth Encounter, Santal Mission, and many congregational owned nursing homes and Bible camps.

ALC Theological Challenges

Lutherans Alert

A small number of ALC congregations and pastors held to a very conservative theological position and became increasingly disenchanted with the ALC. They were convinced the ALC was becoming "liberal." They believed verbal inspiration of the Scriptures to be essential and worried that there was too much social ministry and not enough evangelism. Many meetings were held in pastoral conferences and in conversations with district bishops. Sometimes I was able to take part. Lutherans Alert finally started its own seminary. Those of us representing the ALC used the same testimonies to this group as to the Lutheran Church–Missouri Synod. The group did not attract many congregations and has remained a small group throughout its history.

The same issues were raised again when the decision to merge into the ELCA was made. Again there were numerous meetings and exchanges of views. Ultimately two small groups of Lutheran churches refused to join the merged church and formed new church bodies.

Lutheran Pentecostalism

In the 1960s and 1970s a significant number of ALC members had ecstatic experiences such as speaking in tongues and prophesying. They felt strongly their experiences were the work of the Holy Spirit. There was considerable controversy as others stepped forward to criticize these manifestations. ALC theologians weighed in, some strong proponents of Lutheran pentecostalism and others opposed to the movement. A gathering of congregations and individuals formed a "Fellowship of the Holy Spirit" but remained loyal to the ALC. I spoke at one of their annual gatherings, affirmed their place in the ALC, and urged them not to become judgmental toward others as a result of their experiences. Gradually ALC congregations have became accustomed to having Lutheran pentecostals in their midst. The movement has stabilized and become a part of the Lutheran landscape.

Divestiture

The ALC General Convention, Church Council, Board of Trustees, and Office of Church and Society faced the question of whether to use ALC stock holdings to pressure companies to act against apartheid in South Africa. There was always agreement in the necessity to oppose apartheid. The question was, would a particular action be effective? Did the ALC have the research capacity to provide actionable information? Should the church take actions that are contrary to the policies of the U.S. government? The underlying theological question, which frequently surfaced, was whether the church was called to attempt to influence the policies of secular governmental or private institutions. The theological case for the church to act against manifest injustices in the political or business realm had to be made again and again There would have been no prophetic word against gross injustice if the churches remained silent in the case of apartheid. The ALC followed the lead of the LWF in declaring opposition to apartheid to be a matter of *status confessionis*, a state of confession, an action I strongly supported.

Theology in Dialogues

I was very enthusiastic about ALC dialogues with other non-Lutheran bodies. Historically, inability to reach theological agreement had caused churches to distance themselves from one another. Starting in early Christian history, the refusal of participation in the Lord's Supper on the grounds of theological disagreement became standard practice. Initially the disagreements were profound. The doctrine of the Trinity and whether Jesus was both true God and true man are illustrative. The development of the churches of the West and East led to a lengthening list of heresies. Refusal to share the Lord's Supper with perceived "heretics" became standard practice. That practice has prevailed as Christians have gathered in different confessional groups. Some of the doctrinal disagreements which led to the separation of believers at the Lord's table have become more and more remote from the central articles of the Christian faith. The ALC, together with other Lutheran churches in the LWF, began looking at what was "sufficient" agreement for church bodies to declare themselves in altar and pulpit fellowship. I was among those who thought Lutheran theology should be leading us into closer relationships with other Christians.

Theological dialogues have helped us to draw closer together. The dialogues with other Protestant groups have been simplest, of course. There are differences in Lutheran and Reformed theology that make it useful to maintain different organizational forms, but there is no need to act as though any church has exclusive rights to the Lord's table. In recent times the practical fact has been that Protestants welcome each other at the altar, but not officially. As one of its last acts before the 1988 merger to form the ELCA, the ALC voted altar and pulpit fellowship with Reformed Christians, thus making it an official as well as a practical reality. There is now no reason for the two groups to separate at the Lord's table. It was my hope and expectation that mutual recognition would quickly spread to include the broadest possible range of Christian churches.

The theological discussions with Episcopal representatives were hung up on the issue of apostolic succession. As a practical matter neither Lutherans nor Episcopalians refused communion to each other. Officially, however, the churches were not in altar and pulpit fellowship. It was difficult to get over the official hump because the Episcopalians required ordination into what is called the historic episcopacy. The ALC sought altar and pulpit fellowship on the premise that the two church groups could accept each other "as we are." An accommodation was found that was termed "interim eucharistic sharing." This was done in the expectation the churches would sooner or later find a way to make the relationship complete. It should be mentioned too that the Episcopalians played an important part in changing language from "altar and pulpit fellowship" to "full communion." The ELCA has subsequently accepted a compromise official solution that enables Episcopal and Lutheran inter-communion with the blessing of both church bodies. Installation of ELCA bishops are now expected to include an Episcopal bishop participating in the service. ELCA pastors are then expected to be ordained by an ELCA bishop. Exceptions can be made, however.

The apostolic succession matter is one of the issues that prevents Roman Catholic and Orthodox churches from practicing inter-communion with Lutherans. Apostolic succession, with its hierarchical ordering of the church, will be a cause of theological dispute for the foreseeable future. My conviction is that Lutherans should assert and defend their understanding of the church but not make it a reason to reject others at the Lord's table. It is, after all, the Lord's table.

CHAPTER FIVE

EVIDENCES OF U.S. LUTHERAN UNITY

Personal Ecumenical Experience

When taking office as ALC president, I brought several understandings regarding the unity of the church.

1. That the oneness of the church, the body of Christ, should be evidenced openly in the life and mission of Christian individuals, congregations, and church bodies without waiting for total agreement.

2. That the attitudinal changes in local, national, and international communities of Christians following World War II was widespread, stunning, and compelling. Protestants, Roman Catholics, and Orthodox were affirming each other as sisters and brothers in the faith rather than as heretical opponents.

3. That U.S. Lutherans should affirm their oneness in Christ through active ecumenicity, first with fellow Lutherans and then with all of Christendom.

4. That the ALC and LCA were already living in functional unity with mutual commitment to the Lutheran Confessions.

5. That the ALC, LCA, and LCMS needed each other to affirm their unity as churches of the Lutheran Confessions. Conflicted U.S. Lutherans could not make their best contribution to the life and mission of Christ's church.

6. That important differences in doctrinal convictions should be dealt with as debates within the household of faith rather than as reasons for refusing fellowship.

The president of the ALC served as the church's ecumenical officer. It was a huge task which, along with the duties described in the section Church in the Public Square, claimed approximately one-third of my time. There was a mountain of work to be done with other Lutheran churches and with the wider family of Christian churches. As president of the ALC, I was deeply engaged with U.S. Lutheran ecumenism from my first day in office. In addition, as ALC president I was deeply involved in global ecumenism as a member of the governing bodies of the Lutheran World Federation (LWF) and the World Council of Churches (WCC). These ecumenical bodies gave expression to unity in Christ across church body lines, national boundaries, and confessional differences. My predecessors as president of the ALC, Fred Schiotz and Kent Knutson, had provided strong leadership for these ecumenical bodies. I sought to follow in their train. The breadth of ecumenical activity will become obvious throughout the remainder of this book.

Ecumenical activity was an integral part of my pastoral life from my first days as a parish pastor. The congregations I served were involved in city and state councils of churches, and I took my participation in such councils as a natural part of my pastoral duties. I had to genuinely reflect on my ecumenical convictions, however, when in 1954 the Evangelical Lutheran Church (ELC) convention was faced with a decision of whether or not to join the World Council of Churches.

Opposition to WCC membership was strong, including opposition from respected clergy and lay leaders and some theological professors. Books and pamphlets were written, and rallies were held around the country at which both proponents and opponents had opportunity to speak. As a church body the ELC had limited its close association to Lutherans. Joining the WCC would be a dramatic change in ecumenical direction.

Convention planners recommended and the convention voted that there would be six speakers for and six against membership in the WCC and then a vote would be taken. I was a young pastor from South Dakota, having been ordained in 1950. I had made known my support for WCC membership at the ELC's South Dakota District Convention and in other settings. I believed strongly that Lutherans needed to be engaged in ecumenical church life in local communities and in the world-wide ecumenical movement. I was chosen to be one of the six speakers in favor of WCC membership.

I remember well the tension in the convention hall. There was broad awareness that a future course for ELC Lutherans was being chosen and that the result would have implications far beyond the ELC. There was both quiet joy for some and deep disappointment for others when the majority of voters declared their conviction that confessing Lutherans should join in the life and work of the WCC. In retrospect it is apparent that subsequent U.S. Lutheran church life would have been very different had the vote gone the other way. The ELC and its successor bodies, the ALC and now the ELCA, have been important participants in WCC life, both as contributors and as receivers.

These early experiences became the ecumenical platform for my service as ALC president. I was convinced that agreement among the churches who professed faith in Christ far outweighed their doctrinal differences. The oneness of the body of Christ needed to be openly evidenced even as important doctrinal differences called for ongoing study and debate. The remainder of these chapters on ecumenism will disclose how this stance informed my ecumenical leadership.

ALC and LCA

Geographic and ethnic differences kept the LCA and the ALC, and their predecessor bodies, from knowing each other well in their early years of church life in the U.S. The LCA through its predecessor church bodies began among the early immigrants to the U.S. A 1962 merger brought together four church bodies to form the LCA: the American Evangelical Lutheran Church (Danish background), the Augustana Lutheran Church (Swedish), the Finnish Evangelical Lutheran Church (Finnish), and the United Lutheran Church in America (mixed background, but predominantly German). The majority of LCA congregations and their national offices were located in the eastern part of the U.S.

The ALC and its predecessor bodies came in later immigration waves and settled predominantly in the U.S. Midwest. The original American Lutheran Church (largely German in background) provided the name for the three churches that merged into the ALC in 1960. The Evangelical Lutheran Church (ELC) was largely Norwegian in background, and the United Evangelical Lutheran Church (UELC) was Danish.

A variety of historical and practical reasons necessitated the two mergers rather than one. However, following the 1960 and 1962 mergers, the LCA and ALC national offices were in constant touch with each other. The parallel national boards and offices of the two churches resulted in many joint efforts. Friendships abounded. Altars and pulpits were open to each other. Pastors and people transferred back and forth freely. As will be indicated in more detail later, I thought the unity of the body of Christ was adequately expressed by the two church bodies. That unity was further expressed in a tri-partite Lutheran Council in the USA (LCUSA).

There were no divisive theological issues between the LCA and ALC. At the same time the two church bodies were not carbon copies of each other. Significant differences in polity and practice existed. The two churches simply ignored those differences and joined forces in a wide variety of ministries. It was taken for granted by most people, certainly by me, that the U.S. Lutheran future would find the LCA and ALC as partners in life and mission. I believed that the unity of ALC and LCA was already an established fact.

Lutheran Council USA (LCUSA)

The ALC, LCA, and LCMS did much important joint work through the Lutheran Council in the USA. The ALC and LCA would have included more joint work under the LCUSA umbrella except that the third LCUSA member, LCMS, would only participate in work which for them did not imply doctrinal agreement. The three church presidents were members of the LCUSA executive committee. In the early life of LCUSA, the opportunity to meet both formally and informally with the LCMS president and other LCMS officers had the LCA and ALC members of the executive committee thinking and hoping that joint membership in LCUSA was the beginning of a steadily deepening relationship among the three church bodies. Planning and enacting LCUSA programs, engaging staff, and setting budgets all served to enhance relationships and provide optimism for the future.

On the program side of LCUSA my greatest involvement was with Lutheran Immigration and Refugee Services (LIRS). LIRS is an independent agency, but it was closely aligned with LCUSA. Every time the LCUSA executive committee met, LIRS would be a major agenda item. Post-World War II resettling of thousands of Lutheran and other immigrants from Europe caused a large buildup of personnel and expertise in refugee resettlement. When the influx of refugees from Europe diminished, LIRS turned its expertise to help the huge number of refugees from other countries, most non-Christian with no previous knowledge of Lutheran churches. Wars, forced exile, poverty, and longing for a better life made the U.S. a haven to millions of refugees from all over the world. Lutherans have played a huge role in the U.S. reception of thousands of refugees from all parts of the world.

The work of LIRS required a great deal of negotiating and lobbying with the federal government in Washington, D.C. LIRS staff people, especially Don Anderson, while managing a large LIRS resettlement program, also were called upon by government leaders for advice and counsel in establishing U.S. refugee policy. They dealt constantly with U.S. officials responsible for refugee policy, including setting limits on the number of refugees to be allowed U.S. entry. The church presidents would be called upon by LIRS staff to urge political leaders to lift refugee restrictions and to assure them that the churches would provide public support for their actions. I met with U.S. ambassadors from the most affected countries, with members of Congress, and with U.S. Immigration Service staff in support of LIRS work. There seemed general acceptance that Lutherans were providing crucial leadership and skilled performance in immigration and refugee resettlement. Proportionate to church membership, the Lutheran churches were leaders in providing resettlement for refugee families.

Another LCUSA program in which I was deeply involved was the military chaplaincy. I had served over three years as an enlisted man and officer in the U.S. Signal Corps during World War II and had experienced the great service provided by the chaplains. Hence I agreed to serve on the chaplaincy committee which negotiated numbers of Lutheran chaplains and provided continuing educational opportunities for them. Each year the military allowed a Lutheran chaplains' conference as a mutual support and educational opportunity. I spoke at two such gatherings, one in San Diego and one near Salzburg, Austria, and found them exceptionally important to the chaplains.

Two other LCUSA programs received my interest and my vote for financial support, but I had no direct responsibilities for them. Theological Studies involved theologians from the three churches. They provided critical biblical rationale for the ordination of women and provided running commentary on what was necessary for Lutherans to enter what is now called "full communion" with other churches. Lutheran Films produced two outstanding full-length movies, *Martin Luther* and *Question Seven*, in addition to various documentaries that were important to the churches.

In my early years in office I thought U.S. Lutherans were steadily drawing closer together and that LCUSA would increasingly be their instrument for joint work. Optimism proved short lived, however, as LCMS enthusiasm and participation dwindled. LCUSA was a noble effort and provided outstanding ministries. It became unnecessary when the LCA and ALC formed the ELCA and LCMS participation in LCUSA ceased.

Lutheran World Relief and Lutheran World Service

Lutheran joint work in support of the world's poor and distressed is a thrilling story. Two extraordinarily strong agencies have made it so—Lutheran World Relief (LWR) and Lutheran World Service (LWS). LWR is a U.S. enterprise supported by the ALC, LCA, and LCMS. LWS is a relief and development arm of the LWF and is supported by its member churches. The LCMS chose not to join with the LWF and hence did not support LWS. However, they were ready to join the ALC and LCA in the ministries of LWR, thus necessitating two agencies. Famine relief, medical services, agricultural assistance, educational opportunities, training of indigenous staff, disaster relief, and keeping the needs of the world's poor and oppressed before the wealthy nations of the earth have been immensely useful services. Every year I would address six to eight ALC district conventions. One of the most satisfying parts of that task was to tell the delegates how they and their congregations were joining with other Lutherans to do wonderful ministries for the world's poor and oppressed people.

A deeply meaningful illustration was the story of visiting an LWF feeding center where seventeen youthful (eighteen to thirty years old) Ethiopian Lutherans channeled food and clothes and blankets provided by LWR and LWS during an extreme drought. Over 70,000 people were served by this center, each with a certain day of the month when they could receive a month's supply of wheat, powdered milk, and soybean oil. Most of the recipients were women and children, and all of them were in imminent danger of starving to death. It was sad and yet thrilling to see a mother with two or three small children struggling home with their life-giving food. Able-bodied men were either drafted into the army or were in cities looking for work. There were no cars or even horses or oxen to help carry the food. The U.S. government donated the food; U.S. Lutherans paid the costs of shipping the food and car-loads of clothes and blankets provided by Lutheran congregations. German Lutherans provided huge eighteen-wheel Mercedes trucks to haul the foodstuffs 150 miles inland from the loading docks on relatively modern highways. Swedish Lutherans provided small Volvo all-terrain trucks to haul the food and clothes to the remote feeding center in the Ethiopian mountains. There the young Ethiopians managed the feeding center. Their operation of the center was flawless. I told how LWR and LWS had merged their Ethiopian relief programs with Catholic Charities and how together they had provided necessities for two million people who almost certainly would have starved to death.

It was a joy to tell about the well-digging done by LWS and LWR. Millions of people have suffered without clean water. Water-borne disease has been a huge killer, especially among children. Over the years LWS and LWR have drilled thousands of wells. Tens of thousands of people have lined up with their gourds and buckets to carry fresh, disease-free water to their homes.

There were so many such stories. If a permanent log of earthly doings is kept in heaven, there will be warehouses full of volumes telling of the work of Lutherans and members of other churches who "when they were hungry, fed them; when they were thirsty, brought them drink."

In 1973, during my first year in office, I heard much about the work being done by LWR and LWS and the additional services they could provide with increased funding. I proposed to our ALC convention committee that we recommend a Thanksgiving Hunger Fund and encourage all ALC members to make special Thanksgiving Day offerings to it. The 1974 ALC convention in Detroit had a huge, stage-wide mural of a woman bringing food to a hungry child. The proposal caught on, became an annual event, and has now become a part of ELCA life, providing hundreds of millions of program dollars for the world's needy.

LWR activity also led to the establishment of a Disaster Relief Fund. Its purpose has been to make quick emergency responses to people facing immediate disaster. Hurricanes, tornadoes, floods, earthquakes, and other natural disasters happen without warning. The needs always are immediate. The Disaster Relief Fund has been set up for quick response, and it has functioned effectively since its establishment.

The unity of the ALC and LCA was evident in both its support for pan-Lutheran ministries in the U.S. and also in far-flung ministries of relief and development throughout the world.

Expressions of unity and disunity between the ALC and the LCMS are lengthy and complicated, time and energy consuming, with both hope and disappointment, and complicated enough to call for a chapter of its own.

ALC AND LCMS RELATIONS

Historical Summary

In taking office in 1973, I believed the ALC, LCA, and LCMS needed each other to fulfill the U.S. Lutheran mission. Lutherans who could not live in fellowship with each other would never measure up to their capabilities in evangelism, in the ecumenical church, or as a leaven in the wider social fabric. I believed the three bodies were one in Christ and one in commitment to the Lutheran Confessions. I believed that Lutheran differences were peripheral and should not be the primary focus for Lutheran theology or practice. I envisioned the three church bodies using LCUSA and other partnership vehicles for united efforts to serve Christ, church, and society as usefully as possible. I believed a major contribution could be made to the ecumenical movement as Lutherans acted together. It seemed obvious to me that Lutherans had important gifts to share in church and society and that those gifts could most usefully be shared by the three church bodies living and serving in unity. Their agreements were overwhelming; their disagreements minor by comparison.

All of the ALC predecessor church bodies had some kind of relationships with the LCMS from the time of the high immigration years of 1850-1900. One of the ALC's predecessor bodies, the original ALC, came close to formally entering into altar and pulpit fellowship with the LCMS in the 1920s and even on into the 1950s. Members of both churches were predominantly German, and member congregations were mainly in the U.S. Midwest. However, various impediments kept them from finalizing an agreement, and subsequent events pulled them apart rather than together.

The World War II years and the post-war years that followed brought remarkable change to the U.S. Lutheran picture. Joint work and personal experiences of Lutheran fellowship were widespread. Common use of the English language, the rapid movement of people from one community to another, military chaplaincies, joint relief efforts in war-torn countries, and other factors contributed to familiarity, friendship, and developing trust among U.S. Lutherans. Ethnic identities were beginning to blur, and awareness of a common holding to the Lutheran Confessions was widespread.

A Tri-partite Proposal

Already In 1963, Albert Anderson, manager of the Augsburg Publishing House, and I were delegates to the ALC Southeastern Minnesota District Convention and prime movers in presenting a motion that the ALC invite the LCA and LCMS to join the ALC in establishing a union committee. We believed the three Lutheran bodies should march into the future together. We were aware that the LCA had a long-time commitment to Lutheran unity, and we were also aware of the encouraging friendly moves of many in the LCMS. We thought that even an abortive call for three-way union would be a helpful step toward ultimate expressions of unity. The District Convention voted to recommend it to the next national ALC Convention

In making the 1963 motion, Anderson and I had assumed it would not pass but thought it might help provide impetus for the LCMS, LCA, and ALC to express the unity that we believed already existed on the basis of common commitment to the Lutheran Confessions. We believed Lutherans should provide a theologically sound center movement in local, national, and global ecumenical life. The growing gulf between mainline Protestantism and a more conservative evangelical Protestantism was increasingly apparent and dismaying. Lutherans were not easily identifiable in that divide. Both mainline and conservative evangelical groups stem from an Anglo-Reformed tradition. Lutherans bring a European continental tradition that did not divide along the mainline and conservative evangelical lines.

Anderson and I thought the ALC, LCA, and LCMS Lutherans were all theologically "conservative." Lutheran unity is the result of sharing the same Lutheran Confession that are described in the shorthand statement, "*sola gratia, sola fide, and sola Scriptura*"—grace alone, faith alone, the word alone. I do not know of any Lutherans who do not fully subscribe to the fact that salvation is by the grace of God through faith in Christ. Neither do I know of any Lutherans who do not embrace the

Scriptures as God's inspired witness to that grace and faith. Justification by grace through faith in Christ is not questioned among Lutherans. Lutherans can be argumentative and hold very different convictions from each other when it comes to various social issues and methods of interpreting the Scriptures, yet be solid as a rock on God's gospel. Lutherans are bound together by the Lutheran Confessions, and those confessions are very forthright about God and the gospel. Lutherans are all conservative when it comes to God and the gospel. To keep stretching the term "confessional" to more and more issues that the confessions do not directly address is to guarantee disagreement. The confessions do not speak directly to a host of social questions that may be important but are sub-confessional in nature. Lutherans in all three churches were deeply committed to the core confessional, evangelical, and missionary character of the church and simultaneously deeply committed to care for the well-being of the whole society, especially the poor. That is where Lutherans should stand. The conviction of ALC, LCA, and LCMS confessional solidarity on the issues the confessions actually address was the backdrop for the proposal that Anderson and I proffered.

We further believed that it made sense for the ALC to be issuing the invitation. The ALC was already practicing altar and pulpit fellowship with the LCA and was engaged in serious conversations with representatives of the LCMS. Official relations between the LCA and LCMS were minimal. Hence the ALC was in the best position to issue an invitation.

The proposal met a quiet demise at the national ALC Convention as the ALC leadership dismissed the usefulness of such a move and the convention delegates agreed. It subsequently became apparent, though at the time unknown to us, that ALC and LCMS leaders were doing a great deal of preliminary work toward the establishment of altar and pulpit fellowship between the ALC and LCMS.

During the 1950s and 1960s church body joint actions gave further evidence of Lutheran openness to each other. The LCMS joined the ALC and LCA as members of LCUSA, LIRS, and LWR. Meetings of theological faculties deepened mutual respect and friendship. Plans for a joint service book and hymnal were adopted by all three bodies. There was a growing sense that unity existed among Lutherans and that unity should be expressed in facing the future together.

The positive developments reached a peak when in 1969 the LCMS and ALC conventions adopted the agreement for altar and pulpit fellowship. The agreement meant the two churches shared sufficient unity of doctrine and purpose that members of the two churches could openly declare their unity, that members could transfer back and forth without question, that open communion would be the norm for each other's members, that pulpits could be shared without questions, and that the future would be open to further fellowship initiatives and joint work. The ALC already had such a fellowship agreement with the LCA, so it now seemed possible that the three churches were on track toward a three-way fellowship. At no time did I think of the three churches merging into one organization. The patterns of church life in each body would have made such a move counter-productive. Unity would have to be expressed in reconciled diversity.

The actions of the ALC and LCMS should have created confidence that the two church bodies were moving toward steadily deepening awareness of unity. As events unfolded, there were actions that widened instead of narrowing the gulf between the LCMS and other Lutherans. That change is detailed in the next pages. Now, twenty years after leaving office, I continue to believe that Lutherans will some day get their act together, recognize their shared faith, and express their unity in reconciled diversity. In my judgment U.S. Lutherans have failed to express their confessional unity and bring it to bear on the ecumenical life of the whole church of Christ. Hopefully U.S. Lutherans will learn from the past, leave it behind, and move into the future together as confessional Lutherans, united in mission and vigorous participants in broader ecumenical life.

Committed But Fearful

When I took office as ALC president in 1973, four years after the ALC-LCMS fellowship had been adopted, I was aware that the recently declared ALC-LCMS fellowship had been opposed by a significant segment of the LCMS. The same 1969 LCMS convention that adopted altar and pulpit fellowship with the ALC by a small margin had elected a theologically very conservative LCMS president, J.A.O. Preus Jr. (Jack), my first cousin, also by a small margin. Jack and a phalanx of conservative LCMS members who had been critical of what they saw as ALC doctrinal aberrations were now the LCMS leaders. The ALC membership generally believed the declaration of fellowship was long overdue and was determined to work to sustain and deepen the fellowship agreement between the two churches. Unity in confessional loyalty existed. Passion for the gospel was central to the faith life of Lutheran believers in both church bodies. Lutheran responsibility to make a strong, positive theological contribution to the ecumenical church was to my mind a summons from God. I envisioned the LCMS-ALC fellowship as a crucially important step toward bringing the ALC, LCA, and LCMS to a positive and effective unity in reconciled diversity. A bickering group of Lutheran church bodies, unable to acknowledge each other's allegiance to the Lutheran Confessions, could not make a convincing case for Lutheran theology. Hence I was committed to maintaining and strengthening the fellowship the ALC and LCMS had jointly entered in 1969. I hoped that it would be possible to keep the two churches on the path to deeper fellowship. I believed that Lutherans had distanced themselves from each other by fighting over a variety of sub-confessional issues. It was obvious from the start that a broader view of legitimate Lutheran diversity on sub-confessional issues would have to be accepted by all three church bodies or more separation would be inevitable. In sum, my early days in office found me hopeful regarding a greater expression of Lutheran unity, but also fearful. It was a time of hopeful and fearful uncertainty.

While the LCMS-ALC declaration of fellowship was a great encouragement to prospects for Lutheran unity, there were also troubling elements that deepened the uncertainty. The ALC was in altar and pulpit fellowship with the LCA, and the LCMS was not. The retiring LCMS president, Oliver Harms, had strongly encouraged closer relations with both ALC and LCA and had been instrumental in leading LCMS into LCUSA as well as into altar and pulpit fellowship with the ALC. However, he was defeated for re-election at the 1969 LCMS convention. The new president, J.A.O. Preus, and other newly-elected LCMS officers had not supported ALC fellowship.

Furthermore it was increasingly apparent that there were problems between LCMS "conservatives" and LCMS "moderates." The moderates had held the chief LCMS offices for some years and had always acknowledged that LCMS unity included both conservatives and moderates. Moderates had lived with and worked with the conservatives. There was widespread doubt that the conservatives would provide the same consideration for moderates. That became particularly clear when criticism of Concordia Seminary President John Tietjen became especially heated. It was clear to me that the moderates were just as grounded in the Lutheran Confessions as the conservatives. It would have been more sensible to use the terms "ultra-confessional" and "confessional" to indicate the differences between conservatives and moderates.

I hoped the election of Jack Preus would prove to be a positive development. I had personal reasons for being hopeful. Jack and I had been close friends from early childhood and had attended college together. We liked each other, liked our extended family, and shared extensive history in the ELC, a predecessor body of the ALC. Over twenty-five years had passed since Jack left the ELC for the Evangelical Lutheran Synod (ELS), a quite small Lutheran church that was even more rigidly conservative than the LCMS conservative wing. I had some hope that his views had moderated inasmuch as he had left the "little synod" (ELS) for the somewhat more open LCMS. I thought there was a chance that Jack would want to and would be able to lead an LCMS that would allow the modest theological diversity needed to hold Lutherans together.

When Jack and I began working together as church body presidents, he provided some encouraging signs for closer ALC-LCMS relations. Jack talked as though he had embraced the ALC-LCMS fellowship agreement and was looking for ways the two churches could work together. He assured the ALC and LCA of LCMS support for the joint work in LCUSA.

I wrote the following notes after private conversations with Jack during various LCUSA and other meetings. My notes illustrate why I was able to maintain some hope for continuing ALC-LCMS fellowship.

February 27, 1973

[Jack said,] "There is currently no disposition to make inter-church relationships a fighting point this summer. As of now there is no move to rock the ALC-LCMS fellowship boat."

If Jack is re-elected he will declare a season of peace, seeking to heal the wounds of LCMS. One of the ways of doing so will be to announce two programmatic directions designed to placate the LCMS moderate wing. They are:

1. A call to broader, deeper social engagement in matters of justice—race, poverty, etc.

2. An LCMS change of stance on ecumenism. He would propose a loosening up, an opening to inter-church work, particularly in social justice areas. He believes

the two of us can solve the ordination dilemma which would remove the current difficulty between LCMS and ALC. How, he did not say. My surmise from former discussions is that he foresees orders of ordination so that LCMS teachers and others can have some form of ordination. This would include opening up certain ordained areas for women but would close off the wide open rubrics the ALC presently has. I do not think he reckons realistically if that be the case. I do not think we can back off from the wide open stance even if we wanted to. (And I do not want to.)

April 26, 1973

The ALC-LCMS Committee on Fellowship met at Chicago O'Hare. Jack and I lunched together, and I made the following notes.

1. Jack is even more firmly set in maintaining ALC fellowship.
2. For the first time Jack indicated he and [his brother] Robert are on divergent courses.
3. Three major items at LCMS convention:
   a. The election, bringing to focus moderate-conservative split.
   b. The Concordia Seminary controversy.
   c. The fellowship matter (rescission being proposed by many.)

Jack hopes to win the first two, thinks he will but expects it to be a horse race. He expects also to keep fellowship even if conservatives enable victory on 1 and 2.

   d. Tietjen, president of Concordia Seminary, is going to be publicly fired by the convention in July.
   e. Agreed that if he wins, the ALC and LCMS will be able to "do" some things jointly thereafter. He suggested joint visit to New Guinea to see our joint seminary, then returning to announce some joint efforts in the U.S.

May 12, 1973, meeting of LCUSA executive committee

The LCMS inner politics is dangerous, but Jack seems confident. He foresees a whole (a united) LCMS forthcoming. I find it hard to imagine. His focus is:

1. Win the election.
2. Have the convention dismiss President Tietjen of Concordia (St. Louis) Seminary.
3. Begin four-year term calls for seminary professors.
4. Retire twelve professors, release non-tenured.
5. Set boundaries within which seminary professors must teach, eliminating historical-critical method thereby.

That just does not sound like a peace platform to me. Tom Spitz thinks a split in LCMS Is ahead. I have great regard for the weight of tradition, security, pension funds, etc. and think a split of major proportions unlikely. The inner turmoil can only continue, however, in the face of above.

July 11, 1973

I addressed the (LCMS) convention in the face of a committee resolution to "suspend" fellowship with the ALC. The explanation of "suspend" indicated that it did not mean termination of fellowship. Floor presentation and clarification had not been made, so I had to work with the assumption, affirmed by Jack, that it really means a continuance of the status quo. Time will have to tell.

September 13, 1973

J.A.O. Preus and I had lunch. Jack amenable to finding ways to express togetherness, Interested in wider ecumenical stance. Thinks the old Missouri fellowship-unionism position no longer pertains.

Thinks we can find way around the ordination of women issue.

Indicated possibility of LCMS participation in LWF if it could be done without going through a membership battle.

November 15-16, 1973

> Jack again affirmed permanence of ALC fellowship, LCMS continued participation in LCUSA, willingness to participate in LWF activity, and possibility of his going to bat for LWF membership. Tom Spitz indicated to me privately that he thinks Jack has no idea of the depth of the split he has created nor the depth of the antagonism.

The above quotes just from 1973 give evidence of why I remained hopeful, yet fearful. I was always aware that the chances were not good for a change of course from the LCMS conservatives. It was distressing for me, too, that ultra-conservatives held four of the five LCMS seats on the ALC-LCMS Committee on Fellowship although the purpose of the committee was to implement fellowship. Even so, I believed the sweep of history would move LCMS toward the ALC and LCA, and I thought it important to maintain as strong ALC-LCMS ties as possible.

It was apparent at the 1973 LCMS convention that the LCMS ultra-conservative majority was widening the gap between themselves and the moderates in the LCMS. Their criticism of the St. Louis Concordia Seminary and especially its president became increasingly intense. During the convention a large group of LCMS district presidents asked me to meet with them to discuss the repercussions of Jack's election and leadership, and how the LCMS could stay on an even keel. They were deeply hurt and disappointed that "political" campaigning had entered the LCMS. Their anger at Jack and his chief aides was obvious and visceral. The district presidents told of the organizing that had taken place to get a majority of conservative delegates to the convention, how a system had been set up to communicate with conservative delegates during the convention, and how a virtually clean sweep of moderates from church-wide boards and committees was taking place. The presidents were clutching at straws in hoping that I might have some insight on how Jack could be encouraged to moderate. I told the group that I knew no way to respond to a political takeover other than to mount a stronger political effort. That suggestion was not welcomed. "Then we will be just like them!" was one of the responses I heard. The conservatives had done their work in enlisting conservative delegates. In my judgment there would be no change unless the moderates could enlist a greater number of delegates.

I understand the reluctance to develop an organized political process in a church body. Church tradition for centuries suggested that

God made leadership selections without a political process. In 1970 the ALC was challenged by Pastor Keith Bridston to have an open political process. He ran for the office of president largely on that issue. The development of vying "parties" is hard on unity, and self-aggrandizement seems inappropriate in a church that honors humility. Still, even in the most quiescent national church body there is some kind of informal "campaigning" for particular persons to fill major offices.

The events following the 1973 LCMS convention were hugely confusing and created great uncertainty regarding ALC-LCMS relations. The dismissal of President John Tietjen of Concordia Seminary led to the exile of forty-three of forty-eight faculty and the great majority of the students. This led to the creation of a Seminary in Exile (Seminex) and the formation of a group of congregations and individuals that was called Evangelical Lutherans in Mission (ELIM). When it became clear there would be no ameliorating moves by the LCMS administration, ELIM formed a new church body named the Association of Evangelical Lutheran Churches (AELC).

By 1975 many of the LCMS ultra-conservatives were in full cry to rescind ALC-LCMS fellowship. It was clear by then that the LCMS ultra-conservatives were in complete control and that church body actions to rescind ALC-LCMS official fellowship would be forthcoming. There were a few years of dithering while LCMS entered a "suspended" or "protested" fellowship. There were also efforts by LCMS leaders to have the ALC change course and accept the ultra-conservative LCMS theological positions as the rallying place for Lutherans. LCMS moderates who did not opt to join the Seminex movement, especially a substantial number of district presidents, looked for ways to minimize the damage and make sure there was a continuing place for moderates in the LCMS. Notes I wrote following the LCMS 1973 decisions reflected my continuing conviction that the ALC should maintain as strong a relationship with LCMS as was possible. LCMS was in turmoil, and their convention votes indicated an approximate fifty-fifty division between conservatives and moderates.

January 2-3, 1974, meeting of ALC-LCMS Committee on Fellowship

When we made arrangements for the next meeting and agreed on an agenda and were ready for dismissal, Ralph

Bohlman announced one more item. A letter from Luther Seminary faculty to John Tietjen was then surfaced. Dick Warneck led off with a blast at ALC, wondering if we understood how this complicated fellowship. Then Jack delivered the hottest tirade I have yet heard, threatening to get on the anti-fellowship side if the ALC was going to continue providing ammunition for the ELIM crowd in LCMS.

I replied with some heat, indicating I had no more control over elements within the ALC who were hyper-critical of LCMS than he had over LCMS people who continued to bear false witness against the ALC and myself.

I further pointed out that the ALC seminary faculties are good friends and colleagues of the LCMS Concordia faculty, most of whom face possible job loss. This elicited further response from Jack, Warneck, and Nickel, generally angry and threatening in tone. Jack finished with the declaration that he had to have some help from us if fellowship was to be sustained. He again alluded to his support of fellowship as being decisive at Denver, Milwaukee, and New Orleans conventions. This was vigorously seconded by Warneck and Nickel. At one point Jack indicated he was "about fed up with fighting for fellowship and then having ALC people give the anti-fellowship Missourians ammunition for gunning him."

Ed Fendt plugged in to say that there was no way ALC seminary faculties could be expected to be other than supportive to "moderate" LCMS faculty. After all, as far as he knew, there was no ALC seminary faculty that did not agree with the majority of Concordia faculty.

The fireworks simmered down and we prayed, shook hands, and went home.

January 28, 1974, *The Month That Was*

It is difficult for me to see a way for LCMS to defuse the present tension. They will have to adopt an ALC style of dealing with sub-confessional matters. That is, allow the theological debate to go on without declaring winners and losers, good guys and bad guys. The Confessions adequately cover the essentials of the faith. Lesser matters can be debated in a fraternal spirit.

February 4, 1974, following meeting to interview candidates for LCUSA director

[Jack] would provide no satisfactory answer to my questions regarding a plan for reconciliation and co-existence of opposing parties. He foresees no need for signing loyalty oaths or anything like that. He seems to say that subscription to the "Statement of Principles" will be required of professors in the exegetical disciplines but not elsewhere in the faculty. All they have to do is teach their discipline and keep quiet about historical criticism.

I think it terribly naïve of Jack to think that he can back the situation up to that possibility. The faculty has gotten their backs up, have dared him to convict them of heresy or take them back. They will either have to win, leave, or crawl back in craven fashion. The only possible way for a peaceful resolution is a plan for co-existence, and Jack gives no evidence of interest in that.

March 6, 1974

Jack always sluffs off the negative possibilities and presumes a soon turn for the better. He did today too, but I did not accept it. I told him of my discussions with a significant number of LCMS pastors who have indicated with complete sincerity that they will not go back to the "old Missouri." Jack does not believe that the district presidents, the pastors, and congregations in any number will leave the LCMS. He thinks the mood of the church has swung heavily against the moderate faculty and the rebellious students. However, he for the first time said, "I may be wrong." "I may be looking through rose-colored glasses." "I may be way out in orbit." So at least he has some doubt.

Some of his statements were: "When the seminary faculty went out I thought the Missouri Synod would blow up. Instead there is silence." He told about being at the Atlantic

District meeting when they voted $50,000 to the Seminary in Exile. He saw victory in the fact that they voted it "extra" instead of taking it out of current district income. Also in that John Tietjen had not issued a press release, that assured him that Tietjen viewed it as a defeat. He said, "We are never going to chase down moderate pastors and make them reject the moderate position." However he was very cagey about seminary faculty and some of the national staff. "The seminary board of control has its dander up and will not take just any faculty back. Some of them they will not take back."

I left him with a final statement that there was no way for him to win if he allowed the fight to remain a win-lose situation. There are too many moderates who will never forget the tyranny that made them "losers." He gave one of his indeterminate "yahs," and that ended it. Jack refuses to take my words seriously. He is just an incurable optimist with regard to his position. I believe foolhardily so.

March 9, 1974, at LCUSA annual meeting

I indicated that if it appeared to the ALC that there was no longer reason to be hopeful about LCMS and ALC and LCA converging, that the ALC would be required to go on a union path bilaterally with the LCA. I then asked, "Jack, can you stand up before the world and declare there is room in LCMS for a Lutheran range broad enough to include present conservatives and moderates? Is your theology flexible enough to allow you to do this?"

He never answered the second question. The first he answered, "No." His reasoning was that he would thereby foment a split of major proportions from the ultra-conservative wing of LCMS. The best he could do was to give mollifying ad hoc answers in order to prevent possible splits.

During the LCUSA meeting there was a very pronounced strengthening of official LCMS sentiment in support of the council. After cutting $100,000 from the budget and causing a crisis, LCMS provided $50,000.

March 15, 1975, following LCUSA annual meeting

Jack Preus . . . continues the internal pressure on LCMS moderates. There is no apparent letup in his efforts to whip them into line without splitting LCMS. At the same time he remains as affable, folksy, and friendly as ever. I am grateful that he continues unchanged in his willingness to maintain relationship with other Lutherans. He assured us again that he will introduce nothing to endanger fellowship with the ALC or participation in LCUSA. Stated that way, of course, he can duck the issue if enough strength develops in LCMS to launch a serious attack on either. I doubt he would oppose any efforts that he thought had a chance of cutting off ALC or LCUSA relations.

That is the one change in Jack over the last twenty-five years. Until he became LCMS president he did not allow "unionism." That has changed. He can now pray with us, at least in small meetings. Also, he makes no attempts to undo the fellowship voted with the ALC. I guess that is enough to keep me a little hopeful there may be more bending.

April 16, 1975, lunch with LCMS pastors, Norman Kretzmann and Alton Wedel

The ALC must start planning for the eventuality of an LCMS split. It has increasingly appeared to me that the build-up to intolerability has taken place. Today's luncheon simply confirmed the fact. LCMS pastors Norman Kretzmann and Alton Wedel were guests.

The result is the conclusion that Jack Preus is not going to allow an LCMS in which the historical-critical method will be allowed. I have assumed that when things get tough enough, especially when the money pinch comes, that Jack would accommodate. I no longer believe it. The money crunch has come, the LCMS bitterness level has gone over the top, and he has made no move at all. I can only conclude that he is prepared to pay the price, whatever it is, for absolute allegiance to a rigid literalism with "inerrancy" being the key word.

This will require a new strategy for the ALC. We have been functioning with three fundamental presuppositions that undergird our actions, or lack of it: 1) That the three large confessional U.S. Lutheran bodies should accept each other in altar and pulpit fellowship. 2) The worst thing that can happen to U.S. Lutheran unity is an LCMS split. A remaining strong, ultra-conservative LCMS spending generations pointing accusing fingers at the rest of us Lutherans is a distressing prospect. 3) The ALC at all costs must keep the LCMS fight from becoming an ALC fight as well. We are ready for full front-line mission, united and enthusiastic. To be sidetracked into a hermeneutical squabble would be pitiful.

It is impossible to simply leave LCMS moderates to their fate, however. Some word has to be spoken that will identify with them. That is the problem to be faced now. With the Anaheim LCMS convention coming up in July it will have to be an incisive word.

The above quotes disclose several things:

1. My consistent efforts to hang on to ALC-LCMS fellowship.
2. Jack's continuing assurance that he sought to implement fellowship, even though there were often actions that made it difficult to believe.
3. A strong LCMS minority indicated their intent to stand with ALC and LCA.
4. Another strong LCMS minority sought an end to current LCMS-ALC fellowship.

Official Fellowship Ended

The LCMS vote to end ALC fellowship came in 1981, twelve years after it was first passed. The majority vote to end the fellowship was just about the same percentage that initially enacted ALC fellowship.

The fellowship with the ALC had been a problem for the new LCMS leadership, but it had not been their greatest problem. The greater problem for the ultra-conservative Missourians was their inability to accept the large segment of LCMS that was identified as moderate. For many years LCMS conservatives and LCMS moderates were uncomfortable with each other. The moderates were always willing to live and work with the conservatives, and had done so for many years when holding the chief offices. The ultra-conservatives were not of a like mind. I felt certain that if Jack had a mind for it he would be able to convince the conservatives that they could live peaceably with the moderates. I am not sure that was true but would have bet on Jack if he tried. It was apparent that, if the LCMS could not make peace among themselves, the LCMS-ALC fellowship agreements would founder. The rancorous split in the LCMS ranks made it clear that official fellowship relations between the ALC and LCMS would not last.

The four primary theological issues that led to the LCMS ultra-conservative leadership's rejection of continued fellowship with the ALC were the inerrancy of Scripture, the use of the historical-critical method in interpreting the Bible, the ordination of women, and the practice of unionism. The LCMS thought these matters definitive for church fellowship while the ALC thought they were not. LCMS leaders insisted that the ALC was theologically in error in allowing those practices, thus forcing the LCMS to declare that church fellowship should not be practiced. ALC leaders held that there was no biblical or confessional warrant for claiming that differences on such matters should be church divisive.

For brevity's sake I offer a simplistic look at each of these issues. The LCMS ultra-conservatives argued that the rejection of inerrancy and the use of the historical-critical method made the Bible just like any other book that could be analyzed and picked at in ways that would ultimately place the entire Christian message in doubt. They saw it as undercutting the truth as disclosed in the Bible and in the Lutheran Confessions, and they believed that the inerrancy of Scripture and rejection of the historical-critical method was the way to protect the truth. ALC representatives thought that responsible Bible students ought to use the best available interpretive tools in order to bring the greatest possible clarity to the biblical word. ALC people believed that using the best possible critical tools would strengthen biblical witness to the gospel.

Women's ordination was seen by the LCMS to be a rejection of biblical authority inasmuch as the Apostle Paul clearly states in the Scriptures that "women are to keep silent in the church." ALC representatives pointed to theological studies carried out over several years by theologians from the ALC, LCA, and LCMS which concluded that a study of all the Scriptures leaves the church without a definitive biblical word as to the ordination of women. It is seen as a matter of the church's best judgment. The two LCMS theologians on the study committee split at the end of the study. One affirmed the study, and the other refused. The LCMS officially remains ardently opposed to women's ordination

Unionism by one name or another has been a problem for Christians since the apostolic era. The LCMS held that any deviation from doctrines held by the LCMS was church divisive. Therefore it was wrong to join other Christians in sharing the Lord's Supper, being in the same congregation, or even praying together. To do so was to practice unionism, falsely suggest that agreement exists, and thereby fail to give clear testimony to the truth. The ALC maintained that it was wrong to make doctrines that are not clearly expressed in either the Scriptures or the Lutheran Confessions determinative for church fellowship. Further, there was growing awareness in the ALC that the use of the Lord's table as a disciplinary device was wrong-headed no matter how long it had been practiced.

The LCMS and ALC and predecessor bodies wrestled with these problems for decades. Even so, and in spite of the LCMS 1969 vote to officially enter fellowship with the ALC, these issues remained contentious in the LCMS throughout the following decade.

After the split in LCMS had resulted in a complete conservative takeover, I penned a note to myself about what I viewed as the LCMS debacle. Writing of the turmoil in the Lutheran Church–Missouri Synod I wrote:

> There is a deep concern registered again and again for the LCMS. There is no question that the ALC sympathies are overwhelmingly with the (LCMS) moderates. Very few can see any reason for the heavy handed actions against them.

> The only conclusion I can come to is that the conservative Missourians have committed themselves to total victory. They seek to drive out their presumed opponents. Apparently there is no room for dissent, no debate except with a winner-loser result, no unity with diversity. Uniformity is the goal. Lockstep theology with an infallible LCMS convention determining what the totally correct theology shall be. No thanks!

In bringing a greeting from the ALC to the LCMS at their convention in 1975, I likened their view of a proper church body stance to a clear soup. No matter where you put your spoon you are supposed to be able to get exactly the same texture and taste. Then I likened the ALC to a fruitcake with a variety of ingredients, including a few nuts, with special tastes and texture that formed a very tasty whole. The moderates received the comparison with glee, but the conservatives were predictably quiet.

Throughout the turmoil in the LCMS I had numerous conversations with leadership from the LCMS moderate wing—LCUSA Executive Secretary Tom Spitz; District Presidents Griesse, Zeile, Behnken, Mueller, Hecht, Lieske, Simon, Prokopp, Jacobs, Ressmeyer; LIRS committee chair Pastor Gus Bernthal; and pastor friends Harry Huxhold and Ralph Moellering. In a particularly telling conversation with Dr. Fuehrbringer, former president of Concordia Seminary and one of the Seminex exiles, I asked how the LCMS could accept Jack and Robert Preus as theological professors given their previous antagonism to the LCMS. His response was the sense that Jack and Robert were moving in a moderate direction and that participation in the LCMS seminary faculties would hasten that movement. When I asked if he had requested information about them from ELC seminary faculty or others he responded that "to his regret" he had not. Equally confusing for me was the word from Pastor David Ylvisaker, an LCMS pastor who moved into the ALC, that Professor Carl Piepkorn had recommended Robert Preus for the Concordia Seminary faculty. If that is correct I cannot imagine what could have led Dr. Piepkorn to such a point, given his usual moderate proclivities.

After the LCMS conservative takeover was completed in 1975, the ALC and LCMS continued a joint Commission on Fellowship that met once a year to maintain a liaison and register concerns. Jack and I served on the committee. Jack's choices for other LCMS representatives came from the farthest possible "right" of the LCMS conservatives. Kurt Marquardt, Theodore Nickel, and Karl Barth made Jack look moderate. ALC representatives such as former seminary president Ed Fendt and seminary professors Duane Priebe, Roy Harrisville, and John Stensvaag maintained a serious and friendly theological contribution and refused to get into a shouting match with LCMS counterparts.

In sum, I consider the split in the LCMS to have been a Lutheran tragedy, the most unhappy intra-Lutheran event during my years as parish pastor and church body president. It put the focus on Lutheran squabbling and a resultant failure to make the strongest possible evangelical witness to both church and society. Lutherans could have brought the Lutheran Confessions that transcend the "conservative" and "moderate" divide into the center of national and international ecumenical life. In my mind a huge opportunity was missed.

In the course of the ALC and LCMS relationship, I came to represent in Jack's mind a Lutheranism that had gone doctrinally astray. In like manner I thought Jack represented an ultra-conservative rigidity that departed from the best of the Lutheran heritage. The great difficulty was that the ALC could live in fellowship with both moderate and conservative Missourians, but the conservative LCMS could not live in fellowship with the conservative and moderate ALC. I grieve that theological intransigence on sub-confessional matters prevented U.S. Lutherans from moving into the future together. I believe we missed a great opportunity to express the unity that exists.

While fulfilling our respective responsibilities, Jack and I came to an unwritten agreement that we could assert our differing convictions openly in the meetings and elsewhere, but that we would remain civil and friendly kinsmen, brothers in Christ in spite of our differences. It was sometimes clumsy, but it worked. I remain deeply sorry that Jack could not accept Lutheran boundaries broad enough to include all Lutherans committed to the Scriptures and the Lutheran Confessions.

CHAPTER SEVEN

MOVEMENT TOWARD MERGER

ALC and LCA

The expectation that the LCMS was ending participation in LCUSA and fellowship with the ALC served to heighten the expectation of closer ties between the ALC and LCA. In both the ALC and LCA there was a weary sense that there was no foreseeable point when LCMS would be ready to acknowledge the solid Lutheran confessional faith shared by ALC and LCA. It was time to face a Lutheran ecumenical future without LCMS participation.

There was a long history of merger talk between the LCA and the ALC. The ALC had been formed in 1960 by a merger of three Lutheran churches, the LCA by a merger of four other Lutheran churches in 1962. There was some talk at that time of uniting all seven of the merging churches into one new church, but that proposal gained no traction, and the ALC and LCA were formed. There were no theological impediments to a seven church merger, but the historical and practical realities made it too difficult to envision. The two churches resulting from the 1960 and 1962 mergers worked closely together, however, both through LCUSA and joint actions of various parallel program units.

I came into the office of president convinced that massive organizational re-structuring of church bodies is difficult, painful, and too often with little gain. That conviction resulted from participation in previous restructuring of large organizations, especially in a previous ALC restructuring. I came away from that experience with the conclusion that massive restructuring was expensive, distracting, time consuming, and with little pay-off compared to the cost. I had argued that ALC and LCA unity goals could be met by an ongoing "tinkering with the machinery" that would allow incremental changes to be made without requiring a major disruption in mission. I thought there was a widespread merger fever fueled by unreal expectations.

In my several years as ALC president I was increasingly aware of very substantial polity differences between the ALC and LCA that would make it impossible to have a simple and seamless transition into a new church organization. I believed a merger would be complicated, difficult, and costly, and that it would exact a price for years to come. I believed unity existed in the ALC and LCA relationship. Both churches were functioning effectively, working together closely, and maintaining a positive outlook for the future in the face of widespread social disruption. It seemed wise to me that the churches should make organizational changes in a piecemeal manner when it was clear that greater effectiveness in mission would result.

In 1975 the LCA and ALC formed a Committee on Church Cooperation. The committee sought to deepen the relationships between the ALC and LCA and engaged in preliminary discussions about merging the churches' foreign missions and pension programs. It also, to my way of thinking, showed that genuine unity could exist without full organizational merger. The Committee on Church Cooperation helped the two churches concentrate on their mission goals without being dominated by talk of merger.

There were two dominant convictions regarding Christian unity that I brought with me into office. One was my conviction that Lutherans were called to express their unity both with each other and with non-Lutheran Christians. I believed Lutherans had too often used their distinctive Lutheran Confessions to unnecessarily isolate themselves. The other was the conviction that God's summons to live in Christian unity does not require a single, all-encompassing organized church body. The prospect of Christian churches going through an endless series of mergers in order to express their unity made no sense to me. It seemed apparent to me that both the ALC and LCA were large enough for each to function effectively, that members of the two churches were moving back and forth in the congregations without difficulty, and that all were invited to share God's grace and the church's unity by coming together at the Lord's Supper. Furthermore I thought both churches were doing effective mission work and doing it together where it improved effectiveness. I believed this to be an adequate expression of the unity of the church.

My thinking was expressed at the 1976 LCA Convention in Boston.

> In LWF, LWR, LCUSA, WCC, and their precursors we have worked side by side for many years. In social ser-

vices, campus ministries, and chaplaincies we do our work together. All our divisions and offices are in close touch with each other and join efforts whenever it is useful. Together we develop a Statement on Communion Practices, together we produce a service book and hymnal, and together we work to alleviate hunger in the world. We are training our pastors together in St. Paul and Berkeley and are working at it in Columbus. That will mean that three-quarters of our ALC seminary students will be trained under joint LCA/ALC auspices. What greater sign of unity, of mutuality, of trust can there be than when churches entrust to each other the training of pastors. Let me say to you right now—you cannot get rid of the ALC even if you want to. The glue is too thick. The ALC is committed to the unity God has given us.

The ALC is committed to joining our work with other Lutheran churches wherever we are thereby more effective in mission. That is what church organization is for—to be effective in mission. We do not believe organizational uniformity is an end in itself. We think it wise to consolidate where it helps mission and leave things alone where thorny organizational problems make it more difficult than it is worth. We do not believe that solid Christian unity requires organizational uniformity.

My reading of the LCA delegates response to my speech was twofold. One, there was genuine appreciation for my strong words for LCA and ALC unity. Two, they remained committed to organic unity as the goal for Lutherans.

ALC, LCA, AELC Deciding to Merge

There were distinct differences of opinion among U.S. Lutherans as to what properly constituted church unity. The LCA and AELC and a significant proportion of ALC people believed that the merging of church organizations into a single new organization was necessary for a truly united church. I argued for a "unity in reconciled diversity" which assumed that the church at its best and most obedient did not have to be organizationally uniform.

The creation of the Association of Evangelical Lutheran Churches (AELC) and its participation in what had been the Committee on

Church Cooperation brought immediate change. LCA and AELC representatives wanted to start right off with a yes or no vote on merger. That had been the consistent position of the LCA for many years, and the AELC followed suit. It was my hope that an ALC majority would see closer cooperation and more joint work as a sufficient indication of the oneness of the three churches. In my mind the unity of ALC and LCA and AELC was already visibly evidenced in mutual acceptance of the Lutheran Confessions, altar and pulpit fellowship, and the extensive joint work of the churches. Enough ALC leaders supported merger of the three groups to require that the Committee on Church Cooperation now be named Committee on Lutheran Unity (CLU).

I and others of like mind tried to promote various options that would create a united church without requiring a massive restructuring of three churches into a single new church body. Suggested options included a gradual approach where units of the church would be merged as it became obvious they could function more effectively by doing so; a simple declaration that we were now one church with three major units, or two units if AELC congregations preferred to identify with either the ALC or LCA; or an official federated union which would enable the continuing function of the church bodies without requiring a disruptive total reorganization. None of these options found sufficient support to make them viable alternatives to total merger. However, the committee agreed to recommend that the three churches study the options in anticipation of a straw poll.

As it developed four options were presented in pamphlet form to ALC, LCA, and AELC congregations in time for consideration before the 1981 district and synod conventions where straw votes would be taken. The options ranged all the way from continuing "as is" to totally merging. It was a foregone conclusion that the AELC and LCA votes would be overwhelmingly for total merger. A real debate took place in the ALC, however. A favorable vote of the ALC General Convention required a two-thirds majority of delegates in favor of merger. It was my hope that the ALC straw vote in the districts would show that substantially less than two-thirds would vote for immediate merger and that, therefore, the three church bodies would continue in their present form and proceed to make changes piecemeal as needed.

Reasons For and Against Immediate Merger

There was vigorous debate in the ALC leading up to the 1980 district conventions. The pros and cons were widely discussed in both formal and informal settings. The following listing of reasons given for and against immediate merger may not be complete, but it does outline the differences.

Reasons for proceeding to merger were:

1. The Bible charges believers to be "one," as especially expressed in John 17. There Jesus prayed that believers might be one as he and the Father were one—that is, as complete a oneness as possible. This requires church bodies to merge into one body wherever and whenever possible. It is seen as a matter of biblical faithfulness. Further, Jesus prayed that we might be one so the world might believe. Complete organizational unity is seen as a strengthening of the church's witness to the world. Anything less than complete organizational merger is seen as temporary, incomplete, and awaiting the ultimate unity. This was the strongest reason in support of merger and, in one form or another, was most often used.

2. Merger would result in the church being more effective in mission. Both human and financial resources would be used more strategically by combining like units of the three churches.

3. Where congregations belonging to one of the church bodies were located in areas where another church body was dominant, merger would facilitate consolidation into one church body, thus ending isolation of some congregations.

4. Merger would end the need to be frustrated by repeated questions as to why there were three independent Lutheran church bodies.

5. Failure of complete merger would imply that sinful division still exists.

Reasons against proceeding to merger were:

1. Unity exists. The unity of the church does not require organizational uniformity. Members of the three churches were moving back and forth in the congregations and doing effective mission work, and all were invited to share God's grace and the churches' unity by coming together at the Lord's table. The suggestion that organizational uniformity is essential fits a Roman Catholic view of the church but not a Lutheran view.

2. Both ALC and LCA were functioning effectively with high esprit at a time when turmoil, membership retreat, and diminished finances were commonplace among U.S. Protestant churches.

3. The different polity and practices in the three church bodies precluded an easy "fit" in a merger. The process to a new merged church would be long, hard, expensive, and would require a slowdown in mission work, loyalty, and esprit.

4. The ALC was formed from a major, three-body merger of 1960. Those three church bodies had been similar in polity. Yet it took several years for the merged church to function at something near peak capacity. To then plunge into another major merger that would be much more difficult than the previous one did not seem good stewardship. The benefits of the previous mergers had not yet been fully reaped.

5. Ethnic divisions had been overcome in previous mergers. A new merger would not significantly affect the diversity of the church.

6. There were no apparent church-divisive theological divisions that needed to be healed.

7. Financial support for national programs was bound to suffer. Shutting down three church bodies and starting up another would inevitably result in seriously diminished mission financing.

I gave voice to these concerns in many ALC settings including through the church-wide periodical, *The Lutheran Standard*. The following quotation from the March 20, 1981, issue is representative.

> Evangelism must be the chief priority for Lutheran congregations in the 1980s. I believe everybody agrees with this priority. Last October, the ALC's general convention overwhelmingly declared that evangelism should be our church's first priority in the years ahead. . . . But a preoccupation with church structure, which a commitment to merger would entail, will not meet the critical challenge that faces U.S. Lutherans and their congregations. . . . We can broaden our expressions of ALC-LCA-AELC unity without undertaking a massive, nationwide structural reorganization. The Committee on Lutheran Unity's "Option 1" is as valid a means of expressing our Lutheran unity as the options calling for merger. Continuing in our present organizational structures is a dynamic option, not a static one.

Our three church bodies continue to find new areas to do joint work without having to dismantle existing organizations and build new ones. The Lutheran Council in the USA, Lutheran World Ministries, and Lutheran World Relief are examples of inter-Lutheran organizations that allow broad-based participation in joint work. We have merged seminaries. We created the Lutheran Social Services system. After years of merging and restructuring we have organizations that are working effectively and are familiar to us. Our Lutheran crisis is not an organizational one.

I can see many possibilities for new joint activity. The AELC, whose congregations formerly were part of the Lutheran Church–Missouri Synod, has indicated its intent to be a transitional grouping. The AELC could join the LCA and/or the ALC in one of several possible ways. I believe we can join our ALC-LCA-AELC world mission efforts without a major dislocation. A single Lutheran Foundation—a joint development program—already is under consideration. . . . Many other avenues for merged activity could be named.

A complicated national union of church bodies should be undertaken only when such action clearly will make the church more effective in mission. We have no biblical or confessional mandate for any particular form of church organization. Jesus' prayer for unity in John 17 is not a directive making organizational uniformity or a single organization the ultimate goal for Christendom.

I am concerned that efforts to merge our churches not dominate the life and work of our congregations and church bodies, making us less rather than more effective. Creating new constitutions, arguing about the best formulation of the doctrine of Scripture, and reorganizing the way the church does its work are not incentives for a ministry of outreach. They keep the focus on our "inside" Lutheran concerns—when it should be on our mission on the outside. Our mission is witness to the world, not creation and maintenance of our organizations.

Past mergers healed doctrinal and personal wounds from former disagreements; they gave the strength of size to what had been many small church bodies; they crossed ethnic lines and created genuine "American" churches.

What about now? Some people would argue that a single, larger church body would reduce duplication and increase effectiveness. In my judgment, both the ALC and the LCA are of a size that allows for effective national church life. It is arguable that a single, larger, more complicated organization would require increased staff, would diminish local participation in the national life of the church, and would diminish the personal character of church life at the very time when people are demanding more of those qualities.

Past Lutheran church presidents favored some mergers but opposed others. I was a vigorous advocate of the 1960 merger that resulted in our present ALC—because I believed it essential to end our ethnic enclaves and I thought the merger would make us more effective in mission. But I think there now are better ways to express ALC-LCA-AELC unity in mission than by total reorganization.

The tally of ALC district votes showed that sixty-four percent of the district delegates supported the move to merge. A case could have been made that the sixty-six percent, two-thirds vote was not attained in this straw poll, and that therefore the ALC should insist that the three church bodies continue in their present form. It was apparent, however, that legalistic insistence on stalling a merger would have been deeply divisive in the ALC. It would have assured that the proponents would keep coming back with new proposals for merger until one passed. Further, I was always aware that I had no reason to consider my thinking infallible and was prepared to join the merger effort whole-heartedly if merger was the will of the churches. Hence I recommended to the ALC Church Council that a recommendation in favor of merger be forwarded to the national convention. The result was a vote at the 1982 ALC General Convention that showed over ninety percent voting yes. From the day of the results of the informal poll I committed to the merger process and sought to help create a united, effective, merged, mission-minded Christian and Lutheran church body.

CHAPTER EIGHT

COMMISSION FOR A NEW LUTHERAN CHURCH

The determination by each of the three church bodies to form a new Lutheran church made it necessary to create a union committee. Representatives of the three church bodies, including the presiding bishops, met to recommend a procedure for planning the new church. A few proposed a small union committee which would function as such committees had in previous mergers. That did not find majority favor. After many suggestions, long discussions, and numerous debates, a recommendation was made to the three church councils. It called for a seventy-member Commission for a New Lutheran Church (CNLC). Provision was made for a set number of representatives from each church body with members assigned by geography, race, and gender. It made for a broadly representative group but meant that many would have very limited knowledge of church body history or practice.

The CNLC met twice a year over a six-year period, from 1982 to 1987, in addition many sub-committees and advisory groups met and made recommendations. It was a complicated and expensive procedure, but a workable plan was prepared on schedule. The plan was approved by the appropriate governing bodies, and a constituting convention was set for the fall of 1987. The recommended name, which quickly gained acceptance, was the Evangelical Lutheran Church in America (ELCA). The completion of CNLC work was a remarkable achievement considering all the knotty problems involved.

It was inevitable that a seventy-person CNLC operating on a relatively short time schedule would make the planning task difficult. The commission was reminded constantly of the need for speed in order to meet deadlines. Another beginning difficulty was worry about retained loyalties to previous church bodies. Constant reference to the ELCA being a "new" church resulted in a preference for something new and untried. Some of us thought we should have been talking more about using common practices from the "old" churches. We thought it would be important to emphasize continuity with the previous church bodies in order to maximize ongoing loyalty, familiarity, and affection. Members had liked the previous churches and needed to see the ELCA as a continuation of the known rather than a venture into newness.

Another beginning rule that some of us thought counter-productive was a ban on caucuses by members of previous church bodies. This created a vacuum that was quickly filled by informal caucuses that became agenda setters and influential beyond their numbers. I was one of those who thought that CNLC members with particular church body histories should have had opportunity to propose actions for the CNLC.

CNLC Hurdles

Primacy of Congregations

The ALC had a history of insistence that the congregation is the basic way that God ministers to gathered believers. In and through the congregations believers receive God in Word and Sacraments and carry out Christian ministry to each other and to the uttermost ends of the earth. Church bodies do not drop down from the sky ready made. Congregations create larger church bodies to express their oneness in Christ, to provide services to congregations, and to carry out God's global mission. Hence the ALC's view of the church was reflected in an ALC constitution identifying the ALC as "a union of congregations." I represented the ALC view vigorously to CNLC not just because it was an ALC view but because I believe the congregation is the basic organization of the church and should be known as the primary form of the church.

The LCA identified itself as a "union of congregations and clergy." Clergy members were members of the congregation, but they also had a place in the church's life that was separate from being a member of a congregation. Clergy could elect their own representatives to some church offices. A certain number of seats on the LCA Church Council, for instance, were held for bishops and were not subject to general vote. The LCA saw the clergy with a unique calling not dependent simply on the congregational call. Ordination was dependent on a level of church life beyond the congregation.

As a generalization, we from the ALC saw a special status for clergy as a dilution of the Lutheran understanding of the priesthood of believers. We believed the sense of responsibility for the functioning of the larger church should rest in the congregations and that any church offices outside the congregations should be accountable to the congregations. To see the clergy in a special category in some way independent of the congregations was contrary to our best judgment. In the ALC the districts (synods) were not incorporated. They were functional offices of the ALC at large. In addition, no national staff, including bishops, could be voting delegates to either district or national conventions. The ALC was determined that insofar as possible it should be clear that the congregations, including the pastors, were in charge of the church's life and mission. A further indication of the primacy of the congregations was the ALC system of financial support. Each congregation determined how much of its benevolence money should go to the district for its work and how much to the national church. It was the congregations that determined the support level for the church body.

A formula of congregations and church bodies being dependent, independent, and interdependent developed. At the start of the last CNLC meeting those of us concerned with congregational centrality had managed to retain a sentence declaring the congregation to be the basic unit of the church. That sentence was removed before the final CNLC recommendations were presented. The dependent-independent-interdependent formula was for some of us a formula for shaping an independent national church body with no direct line of accountability to the congregations. We believed this action would distance the congregations from the national programs of the church and tend toward a heavily clergy led church body.

Working Style

Robert Marshall, predecessor of Bishop James Crumley as president of the LCA, was a member of CNLC and a good friend and colleague. We discovered a mutual concern that the CNLC might propose a merged church structure that would owe more to American corporate structures that to the uniqueness of the church.

After as much conversation as we could find time for, we proposed to the CNLC an organizational structure that we thought would be useful for a church body approximately twice the size of either the LCA or ALC. It was a preliminary offering and sketchy, but we thought it worth CNLC consideration. In our thought it was crucial that congregational members experience a strong sense of closeness to, ownership of, and loyalty to the national church body, and we thought that would not be an automatic outcome for the ELCA. We looked for ways to bring decision making and pastoral services as close to the congregations as possible. We sought to make the working of the church as personal as possible to the congregational members.

Our recommendation focused on major regional groupings as the basic expression of a national church body with numerous small synods serving a primarily pastoral function. Regional offices could much better respond to and build on unique regional differences that exist in American society without requiring all the other regions to concur. With regional conventions replacing both national and synod conventions, we saw the possibility for much more personal participation in the church's work. We looked for structures that would help create a communion of all members of the church body and not be experienced as a highly centralized corporate entity. The goal was a very personal, pastoral, close-knit, mission-minded grouping of congregations.

Our plan's primary differences from previous church bodies were:

1. The creation of nine regions with offices that would assume most of the duties previously carried out by the national church offices or by synods. Each region would have a bishop. The congregations in a given region would have opportunity to know personally one of the nine top officials of the church, the bishop of the region. A large number of small synods would be formed whose ministry would be pastoral and not programmatic.

2. National and synod offices, staffs, and boards would have radically different roles. Most of the church body work would be done through the regions. The national offices would be downsized with most of the programmatic work assigned to regions. The synods would be completely pastoral in function.

3. There would continue to be some national offices such as boards of trustees and pensions to provide necessary financial and research services. Regional bishops could provide necessary national leadership on a rotating basis.

4. The synod would be served by a pastoral dean with only secretarial assistance. There would be no administrative or programmatic responsibilities. The dean would provide pastoral services to pastors and congregations as needed and wanted. Administrative and programmatic needs would be provided by the regions.

5. We thought the continuation of previous organizations would encourage the expansion of synod staffs and inevitably the lessening of personal pastoral care from the chief synod pastor. We also believed that to function as the previous LCA or ALC would create a greater sense of "distance" between the congregations and the national offices.

Other CNLC members proposed a working style much closer to that of the previous church bodies, and it was adopted. Marshall and I had not come with a fully fleshed out plan, and that may have been a problem for many. The final CNLC recommended organizational structure included regions and a large number of synods but did not change the roles of national and synodical offices or provide any real role for the regions. Predictably the ELCA has found the regions of little use, and they have either been eliminated or assigned minor tasks.

Ministry

A knotty problem was caused by the AELC considering teachers in their parochial school systems as pastoral equivalents. As in the LCMS, the AELC submitted one list to the government for housing allowance purposes. The list included both pastors and teachers. After much discussion and difficulty, a compromise plan was reached by CNLC.

A strong debate took place regarding the named ministries of the church. Some thought there were only two kinds of ministers, lay and clergy. Others argued for three, lay, clergy, and diaconal ministers.

Ecumenical Commitment

The CNLC created a transition committee to assure the fulfillment of CNLC's plans during the time between CNLC's final meeting and the founding convention of the ELCA. At one of this group's early meetings Bishop Crumley, LCA president, informed the committee that the LCA synod presidents had expressed grave reservations about the merger. There were several expressed concerns, but the chief one seemed to be a worry that the proposed ecumenical statement represented a weakening of the LCA ecumenical commitments.

I recommended to the ALC representatives that the ALC members concur in using the LCA statement on ecumenicity as the recommended wording for the ELCA constitution. The transition team concurred. That apparently had the desired effect, for there were no further concerns expressed by the synod presidents.

Pension Plan

The ALC had a simple, effective pension plan that required congregations to provide a clergy pension by placing in a national pension fund a sum equal to nine percent of the pastor's salary. The fact that there was only one plan for all kept the administrative costs very low. The LCA had adopted a twelve percent plan with a variety of plans from which the pensioner could choose. A U.S. Presidential Commission had recently completed a long study with the conclusion that a nine percent figure would provide a pension that was seventy percent of the last previous income. It also reported that seventy percent should be adequate income for a retired person and therefore recommended those figures for government planning purposes.

I argued vigorously for the nine percent contribution on the grounds of the commission's conclusion of adequacy and because I thought that increasing the pension funding would correspondingly diminish the moneys available for other mission initiatives. All the ALC congregations would have to increase their pension payments, and it seemed obvious it would have to come from their regular apportionments to national programs. The CNLC tried to find some middle ground and recommended a plan that would have capped the ELCA pension contributions at some level between nine and twelve percent. After the ELCA was formed there were efforts to go to twelve percent, but the final determination was ten percent of the pastor's salary.

A further complication was that the ALC's pension plan was totally funded while the LCA's plan did not include funding for retirees health programs. That meant the ELCA would be faced with a very large financial burden in totally funding that benefit. The funds would have to come from the congregations' benevolent contribution and increased congregational pension assessments, and it would be a continuing cost item for decades. This also would diminish funds available for mission outreach.

It is always difficult to establish what a fair and adequate pension should be. I thought the nine percent was fair and adequate and did not like the flat twelve percent. Across the board percentage increases always mean that the much more sizable increases go to those who had received the highest salaries. I thought that if there were to be additional funding for pensions and benefits it should be weighted in favor of those pension fund members who had labored through their working years for very low salaries. The ten percent minimum is now established, and I settle for the knowledge that ELCA pensions will be generous without being extravagant.

Church Council Representation

The ALC sought to keep decision making as close to the life of the local congregations as possible. Hence each district elected two delegates, a lay person and a parish pastor, to serve on the ALC Church Council. District bishops and ALC staff persons were ineligible to serve on the Church Council in order to assure that decision-making could not be in the hands of church officials. The LCA national committee nominated persons for election to the Church Council, and both bishops and other staff members were eligible for election. In a close vote the LCA pattern was adopted for the ELCA.

Quotas

The ad hoc caucuses spearheaded a successful effort to establish racial and gender quotas in the election of delegates to ELCA assemblies. The proposed racial quota called for ten percent of the delegates to be persons of color. I thought that an unwise move because it gave ten percent of the seats to less than two percent of the ALC membership. However I did think it would be wise and fair to make some special effort to increase the number of delegates of color. At one of the CNLC open meetings where delegates were free to float proposals that would not be formal motions included in the minutes, I suggested an alternate plan where the quota would be set at one percent above the actual proportion of ALC members of color. That would have provided a modest increase in the number of delegates of color but would not have set the quota at such a high level as to seriously impinge upon the opportunities for majority members to be chosen as delegates. I believe the suggestion gained no support in the open session because heated debate was already occurring around the question of whether or not there should be quotas at all.

An Opportunity Missed:
Location of ELCA National Offices

Selection of a site for the national offices of the ELCA was on the agenda from the very beginning. Unfortunately the best option by far was doomed from the start, namely, that the new offices should be located in Minneapolis. The initial site selection committee had recommended

Minneapolis, but the CNLC quickly put that motion to rest. Most of the LCA and AELC delegates and some of the ALC would not hear of the new offices being placed in a city that had been home for a previous church body. Their reasoning was that there should be no identification of the national offices with the sites of the previous church body offices in order that there would be no suggestion of a favored position for one of the three merging bodies. Further, they argued that Minneapolis was not a world-class city and that its air service was not comparable to that in larger metropolitan areas. I suspect a further decisive reason was the feeling that LCA predecessor church bodies were the first to be established in the U.S. and had been the most dominant U.S. Lutheran group both in numbers and national significance. Understandably they felt the new church offices should reflect those realities.

On other grounds Minneapolis would have been ideal. It is located in the center of the largest concentration of Lutherans in the U.S. Church members' awareness of national programs would have been significantly better. The ELCA early years were very difficult because of the lack of funds. The financial savings of a Minneapolis location would have been dramatic, in the many millions of dollars. Ideal physical facilities were available. A fine building, former home of a Vocational High School, located within 100 yards of both the very large Central Lutheran Church and the new Minneapolis convention center, was available at a fraction of the cost of the building finally purchased in Chicago. Knowledgeable, experienced ALC staff would have been available for service without the expense of moving. I thought LCA staff from New York and Philadelphia would have been more inclined to accept positions and move to Minneapolis than to Chicago. Those of us who traveled a great deal out of the Minneapolis airport felt there were air travel advantages at least comparable to advantages present in Chicago. It very quickly became apparent that Minneapolis would not be chosen. A different location was necessary, and the decision was made to locate in Chicago, although not without a strong challenge from Milwaukee.

CHAPTER NINE

U.S. ECUMENICAL RELATIONS

National Council of Churches

A brief word needs to be said about the ALC and the U.S. National Council of Churches (NCC). ALC predecessor church bodies did not join the NCC; neither did the ALC when it came into existence in 1960. There was no strong push for the ALC to become a member of the NCC, and the NCC was little known among ALC congregations. Intra-Lutheran ecumenicity was new enough that there was little interest in entering broader alliances. Also, one of the ALC predecessor church bodies had a contentious history with regard to joining the World Council of Churches and had joined that council only in the 1950s.

I gave serious thought to recommending that the ALC join the NCC but decided against it. My reasons were twofold. One, there were still enough ALC pastors and laity who had vigorously and successfully opposed membership in the NCC in years past. I thought it would be unnecessarily distracting to have a controversy on the subject. Two, ALC program units were full participants in much of NCC activities. It seemed to me that this fact would inevitably lead to membership and that it could wait until larger consensus support developed. When the ELCA merger came into the planning picture, it was clear that with the LCA already a NCC member it would be pro-forma for the ELCA to join. That is what happened and with no significant opposition.

Altar and Pulpit Fellowship with Reformed Churches

A Lutheran-Reformed dialogue made steady progress during my years in office, including a recommendation that the ALC declare altar and pulpit fellowship with the Reformed Church in America and the Presbyterian Church USA. Lutherans in Europe had already established such fellowship through the Leuenberg Agreement. I strongly supported the dialogue group's recommendation. The ALC Church Council recommended approval to the ALC convention in 1986, and fellowship was declared at the last ALC convention before the merger. The United Church of Christ (UCC) was also included in the dialogue group, but I recommended they not be included in the ALC declaration of fellowship. U.S. Lutheran history with the UCC had been quite different from the others. I thought it would be contentious to proceed with a formal recommendation for fellowship with the UCC. That could wait until the ELCA was ready to establish formal fellowship with other church bodies.

Relations with Episcopal Church

My real-life engagement with different views of ministry came in 1969 when the ALC, of which I was vice president, was faced with a motion to use the title "bishop" rather than the previously used "district president." During the debate on the subject I took the floor and made a strong speech in support of using the term "bishop." I remember my main point being that we were only changing a "secular" title for a "religious" title, and that it would involve no change in actual practice. Later I came to regret that the ALC voted to use the term "bishop," and I regret having spoken in support of it. The action had ramifications that I did not anticipate. It simply did not dawn on me that such usage would be seen as a significant move toward acceptance of the historic episcopate. In retrospect I think it helped prepare the way for acceptance of an Episcopal-Lutheran agreement that included a requirement that subsequent installations of Lutheran bishops had to have an Episcopal bishop participating. Such action assured the Episcopalians that ELCA pastors would be "properly" ordained through the historic episcopate. My problem is that it moves Lutherans in the direction of a hierarchical view of the church. Historically, Lutherans have understood ordained ministry to be dependent on a call from a congregation of believers and not on the laying on of hands by a bishop. Lutherans understand the clergy to be *members* of the congregation with a particular call to serve as pastor. The hierarchical view sees ordination in the historic succession as endowing the clergy with special permanent gifts not dependent on the congregation. Once a priest always a priest is a hierarchical mantra, but not for Lutherans. The question becomes whether the governance of the church is to be in the hands of a special hierarchical clergy or in the hands of the whole people of God. The ramifications of these contrasting views are great.

It is my conviction, and I believe a historic Lutheran conviction, that bishops of the church are given unique opportunities to provide leadership for the church, but that it is not because of inherent powers of a bishop. My word to ALC bishops was that they had the Bible, the Lutheran Confessions, the ALC constitution, and their powers of persuasion to use in providing leadership for the church.

While there was no established full communion (successor terminology for altar and pulpit fellowship) between the Episcopalians and Lutherans during my years in office, there were actions that provided for an "interim sharing of the Eucharist." Many, probably most, congregations were ahead of national church practices. Sharing at the Lord's table between Episcopalians and Lutherans was commonplace at the local level.

Relations with Orthodox Churches

The relationship with the Orthodox receives a great deal of attention in later sections on the Cold War and nuclear disarmament. Hence I will only mention here that U.S. Lutherans entered into a dialogue with the U.S. Orthodox. I served as co-chair of the group, and we made a start. We were strange to each other both socially and theologically. The Orthodox are much more tied to the early centuries of the church, with liturgical life and a variety of practices that are strange to Western Christians. The Protestant Reformation did not touch them. There was a strong desire to build on the newly established friendships and move into the theological arena. That will take time, however, and the Orthodox think that anything worth addressing will require study and discussion for decades if not centuries. As a generalization, the Orthodox and ALC congregations did not live in geographical proximity to each other so there was not the same sense of ecumenical urgency as with other Christians.

Relations with Roman Catholic Church

The 1963 Vatican Council was an ecumenical landmark. The explosion of ecumenical warmth that followed Vatican II was testimony to the pent-up longing for mutual recognition on the part of both Roman Catholic and Protestant Christians.

ALC ecumenical participation with Roman Catholics has taken place most substantially in the local communities. Before Vatican II most local Roman Catholic and Lutheran congregations had little to do with each other. That changed virtually overnight. Roman Catholics and Lutherans found many ways to express their unity in Christ, their mutual affection, and their shared commitment to doing good works. Joint worship, prayer, and fellowship between congregations became quite common. I often have said that the Protestant and Roman Catholic change in attitudes towards each other in my lifetime has been nothing short of thrilling and the most significant ecumenical happening of the last half of the twentieth century. The change has been personal, internal, and heartfelt, with denunciation and avoidance of each other giving way to friendship and trust. Recognition of each other's faith in Christ was celebrated even as there was frank recognition of continuing deep and difficult differences in important theological matters.

At the national level also the ALC and LCA representatives were involved with Roman Catholics in many settings. The joint theological work done by the U.S. Lutheran-Roman Catholic dialogue was very important in the U.S. and played an important role in the development of international Lutheran-Roman Catholic agreements. Annual meetings between U.S. Lutheran and Roman Catholic bishops have been ongoing and have been marked by solid friendship and mutual willingness to give visible evidence to a shared Christian faith. At one of the joint bishops' meetings at Reformation Lutheran Church in Washington, D.C., there was a joint worship service at which I presided and a Roman Catholic bishop preached.

When Pope John Paul II came to the U.S., I was one of twenty or so Protestant leaders invited to meet with him in Washington, D.C. On the next day Ann and I were invited by U.S. President Jimmy Carter to be part of a welcoming gathering for the pope at the White House. Similar meetings took place in Columbia, South Carolina, at a subsequent visit of the pope. The public gatherings were ceremonial functions, but they provided public affirmation that a new kind of ecumenical era had begun. To underscore that fact and to give a sense of my work as ALC ecumenical officer, I quote from a commendation given when I was awarded the St. Thomas Aquinas Medallion by the Roman Catholic College of St. Thomas at a 1983 college convocation.

> With your approbation and support the Lutheran-Catholic Dialogue continues to progress. Now, as we observe together the 500th anniversary of the birth of Martin Luther, we celebrate our approaching unity, which that

visionary reformer never wished severed. We manifest our faith that God will continue to draw his children together as one in him as we salute you, David W. Preus, and confer upon you the medallion of St. Thomas Aquinas.

Archbishop John Roach of the Minneapolis-St. Paul Diocese, Bishop James Shannon, St. Thomas University President Monsignor Terrence Murphy, Cardinal William Keeler of Baltimore, and a large number of parish priests became my warm personal friends. I cite them as illustrations of a new, positive inter-denominational recognition of mutual membership in the body of Christ.

In spite of the encouraging picture of Lutheran-Roman Catholic relationships given above, I was distressed at the swing back to medieval conservatism on the part of Pope John Paul II. Appointment of the most conservative bishops and rigidity on matters of birth control, ordination of women, celibacy of priesthood, and even issuance of indulgences does not square with a new openness to the thinking of other devout Christians.

Dialogues

The ALC and the LCA were deeply engaged in dialogues with other U.S Christian churches during the 1970s and 1980s. The intent was to find ways to express the measure of unity that existed between Lutherans and other Christians and to find ways to deepen that unity. Joint working teams met once or twice a year. It was quickly and clearly apparent that the churches' common convictions were greater in strength than the things that separated them. Lutherans engaged in joint dialogues with Presbyterian, Reformed, Orthodox, Roman Catholic, Moravian, and Episcopal churches. Opening conversations had begun with Methodist and Baptist church bodies. The groundwork was laid for early ELCA entrance into full communion with the Reformed, Moravian, and Episcopal churches. The Lutheran-Roman Catholic dialogue was difficult but fruitful. Over the years it produced a number of theological papers on which agreement was very substantial. The American dialogue group contributed very significantly to a much publicized international joint Lutheran-Roman Catholic statement on justification by faith.

Inasmuch as I was responsible for ALC ecumenical affairs, I regularly met with ALC representatives on these joint dialogue groups. Mainly I did so to remain current regarding progress in the dialogues, but also as ecumenical officer to make my recommendations to the dialogue groups regarding possible items for consideration. The leaders of the American churches involved met often and both reviewed the work of the dialogue groups and made sure we mutually supported the various agreements reached in the dialogues. My significant contribution was to encourage attention to the areas of agreement as well as the areas of disagreement. It was my conviction that churches had concentrated so much on differences that the sense of communion in the one church of Christ was diminished.

It was exhilarating to experience the great growth in positive assessment of the unity that exists in the churches. It is tempting to think that ALC leaders were trail-blazing ecumenical agents. I think, however, that the ALC's official ecumenical leaders were expressing the theological reasons for the rapid and positive ecumenical change taking place in local congregations throughout the church. The impetus worked both ways: The laity was pushing the national leaders and the national leaders were pushing the laity. Great advances were made in appropriating life in the one, holy, catholic and apostolic church while being honest about the important differences that continue to exist within the one church of Christ.

U.S. Church Leaders

There were other facets in ecumenical work on behalf of the ALC. One of my major concerns was the increasing distance from the so-called conservative evangelical and pentecostal churches. Former ALC President Fred Schiotz initiated meetings of many heads of churches. After a few meetings that group ceased functioning. Milton Engebretson, chief leader of the Mission Covenant Church, and I were instrumental in resuscitating it. We had one immediate goal and one long range goal. The immediate goal was to bring together leaders of both mainline and very conservative churches in order that they might know each other. Mutual friendship and respect is an important initial step in establishing relationships. Long-range hope was that we might contribute toward greater recognition of Christian faith and fellowship across mainline and conservative evangelical lines. An annual two-day informal meeting was held for eight years. It included a broad spectrum of American Church leaders. Mainline Protestant, Orthodox, and Roman Catholic leaders spent informal times with leaders from the conservative evangelical churches and pentecostal churches. Bible studies and frank, free-flowing conversations were held with Bishop Crumley of the LCA, Stated Clerks Bill Thompson of the Presbyterian Church USA and Jim Andrews of the Southern Presbyterians, Avery Post of the UCC, Robert Campbell of the American Baptists, a representative of the Southern Baptists, Roman Catholic Cardinal Bernardin of Chicago, the general secretary of the Southern Baptists, Milton Engebretson of the Mission Covenant Church, Arnold Olson of the Evangelical Free Church, McGill of the Swedish Baptists, and the general secretary of the Conservative Evangelical Council of Churches. Usually twenty-five to forty church leaders took part. A fair portion of them were conservative evangelical, but there were no representatives from the pentecostal churches. There is no way to judge the impact of such meetings, but I see them as a continuing attempt to keep communications open across the denominational divides. The possibilities for ecumenical discovery are immensely greater if people are at least meeting together over common concerns.

I envisioned the possibility of a comprehensive U.S. Council of Churches that could at least witness to faith in the Triune God. Such a new council would include the church bodies presently members of the National Council of Churches, the Roman Catholic Church, as many as possible of the conservative evangelical and pentecostal churches, and of course the Lutheran churches. The possibility of such a gathering of church bodies was a major item for discussion at several meetings. Most of the church leaders thought it was a good idea and encouraged Engebretson and me to keep pushing it. However, the sparks of interest did not become a flame. After a few years it became obvious that few believed it could happen, and the meetings again ceased.

CHAPTER TEN

GLOBAL ECUMENICAL RELATIONS—LWF

Introduction to LWF and WCC

The intent of the ecumenical movement is to express the unity of the church through joint worship, fellowship, and mission with Christians from all over the world. On the global level the people of the ALC were full participants in the life and work of two major global ecumenical bodies, the Lutheran World Federation (LWF) and the World Council of Churches (WCC). The LWF and WCC enabled member churches to experience the existing level of unity of the one, holy, catholic, and apostolic church while seeking ever wider unity through useful service to the whole creation. There were many world-wide ministries the ALC could not attempt by itself. To illustrate:

The ALC by itself could not have maintained strong programs to and with churches behind the Iron Curtain. The ALC could not effectively operate its missionary program without cooperation with other Christians. The ALC by itself would have had minor effect on South African apartheid. Joining with other LWF and WCC churches, an important contribution was made to the ending of apartheid. The extraordinary relief and development activities that ministered to millions of starving, impoverished, oppressed, and disheartened people throughout the world could only be done through joint action.

Indigenous churches throughout the world have been founded and nurtured through the ministries of missionaries sent out by individual church bodies such as the ALC and its predecessor bodies. During recent decades many of these indigenous churches have experienced amazing growth and have assumed ever increasing responsibilities. Some of the indigenous churches now have a membership larger than the ELCA. The growth has been primarily the result of preaching and teaching, first by the missionaries and then by large numbers of indigenous evangelists. Missionary churches such as the ALC helped these young churches by providing backup services, much of it through the LWF and WCC. Providing that backup required frequent difficult decisions by the councils' executive committees. It is always heart-breakingly difficult to decide which ministries to undertake when there are so many needs and only a few can be met.

As the church's ecumenical officer, the president of the ALC was necessarily a major participant in the life of the LWF and WCC. ALC's size and financial support assured that the ALC president would be elected to the fifteen-member LWF executive committee and the WCC Central Committee of roughly 100 members. In addition I was elected to be one of five vice-presidents of the LWF and a member of the WCC fifteen-person executive committee. About every seven years the LWF and WCC would hold world assemblies to determine priorities for the ensuing seven years. Between assemblies the executive committees provided governance for the LWF and WCC and were responsible for seeing that resources were used responsibly and effectively. It was difficult and exciting work. The differences in theology, languages, cultures, economies, educational levels, and political structures guaranteed that LWF and WCC work would be difficult. The need for sharing the gospel, assisting younger churches, and providing relief supplies to poor people presented the churches with gargantuan challenges. It also guaranteed the work would be exciting.

Service in those bodies meant much study, establishing of inter-personal relations, attending meetings, and travel. In the line of duty I was in all the continents save the polar regions. I also made visits to a variety of island nations such as Iceland, Formosa, and Papua New Guinea. Almost always there were preaching opportunities, site visits, and planning meetings with indigenous church leaders, ALC missionaries, and ecumenical partners. Establishing inter-church and international ministries always involves bureaucratic stumbling and stances that are not popular in some of the member churches. Yet an immense number of important ministries were effectively performed through them. I believe the ALC congregations served well and were well served through both the LWF and WCC.

I attended meetings in Geneva, Switzerland, site of central offices for both LWF and WCC, at least twice a year. There were two facets to the ALC president's ecumenical work in the LWF and WCC. One was to participate in mission decisions and governance of both councils. The other was to keep ALC congregations informed and enthusiastic about their world-wide mission work through the ecumenical councils.

There were two main reasons for the ALC membership in two international councils. One, it was important to have an over-arching council of fellowship and service that included churches from many different traditions all over the world. The WCC reflected the fact that there is one, holy, catholic, and apostolic church even though there are many very different Christian churches both inside and outside the council. However, the sheer size and the vast differences in theological convictions, cultural patterns, and the politics of the host countries made it impossible to do all the necessary Christian work through a single organization. Hence much work could only be done effectively through smaller confessional groups such as Lutheran, Reformed, and Orthodox. The offices of both WCC and LWF were in the same building in Geneva, Switzerland, which enabled close liaison. The second reason for Lutherans to maintain a separate council was the importance of uniquely Lutheran doctrines and theological studies. Further, the internal politics in some countries would allow the Lutherans to link with indigenous churches but would not allow the WCC to do so.

Later in this book I will discuss the ALC participation and my personal efforts as president of the church body in the search for peace and justice in a world beset with racism, the Cold War, nuclear threats, and environmental disaster. Suffice it to say here that a major portion of those efforts were done in partnership with other churches through LWF and WCC channels. Ecumenical activities across the Iron Curtain always doubled as initiatives for peace in the Cold War. Ecumenical meetings with churches of South Africa and Namibia were always actions against apartheid. In like manner, meetings to combat racism or to deal with war threats were most often ecumenical in character. There is no way to make a clear division between ecumenical activities and peace-making. There are many areas where ecumenism and work for unity, justice and peace are simultaneously involved.

The scope of this book does not allow a broad overview of the two ecumenical councils. Rather, the following pages will give a brief review of some of the many ways in which ALC ecumenical life in the LWF and WCC involved the ALC congregations and president in world-wide ministries. The following descriptions of the work of the LWF and WCC are only illustrative, small pieces of a much greater whole.

LWF Governance

The LWF Assembly that met every seven years, with delegates from each of the member churches, was the ultimate decision making body for the LWF. The assembly reviewed previous work, made decisions important at the time, elected officers, wrestled with constitutional changes, and adopted a broad outline of action for the ensuing seven years. I participated in four LWF assemblies. In Evian, France, I received my initiation into LWF life. The 1970 Evian assembly was marked by the changing of the guard. At the conclusion of decades of leadership following World War II, men such as ALC and LWF President Fred Schiotz and German Bishop Hans Lilje completed their LWF work. It was a moving and historic meeting. Schiotz, Lilje, and others had played dramatic roles in World War II, and we were all aware that it was the end of an exceptionally important era. The new president elected in Evian was Archbishop Mikko Juva of Finland. Juva had the difficult job of chairing the 1977 Dar Es Salaam assembly that dealt with South African apartheid. Election of Bishop Josiah Kibira from Tanzania provided the first third-world LWF president. His election was cause for a great celebration in Dar Es Salaam. The 1984 assembly in Budapest, Hungary, was notable for being the first such gathering in a Soviet bloc country and for electing Bishop Kaldy of Hungary as the first president from the Soviet bloc. The 1990 assembly in Curitiba, Brazil, was the first major LWF gathering in a Latin America setting. I thought the assembly provided excellent program leadership for its missionary and service units and then spent too much time with a divisive proposal for a massive re-structuring of the LWF. After lengthy and heated debate, the LWF re-structuring was passed on a tie vote. Then planning for the next seven years of vital mission took place and enabled Lutheran churches to reach many parts of the world with gospel bread for the soul and earthly bread for the world's poor.

The implementation of the assembly actions and dealing with new matters that would arise between assemblies was entrusted to the various LWF departments, with oversight provided by a fifteen to twenty person executive committee that met annually. There were seven officers—president, five vice presidents, of which I was one, and a treasurer—who served on the executive committee along with eight regional representatives. The executive committee provided program and staff supervision, and dealt with matters that could not await the next assembly.

Serving as one of the officers of the global Lutheran fellowship was much work, but it was exciting work. That was especially so during the years 1977-1984 when Bishop Josiah Kibira of Tanzania was president of LWF. He was limited by Parkinson's disease for most of his term and often asked me to stand in for him. Sometimes it was to speak on his behalf, and often he asked me to chair meetings.

This was especially true at the LWF Assembly in Budapest, Hungary, in 1984. With his strength and voice weakening, Bishop Kibira called on me to chair much of the time. Inasmuch as we were meeting in Hungary, Bishop Zoltan Kaldy of Hungary, with encouragement from the Hungarian government, let it be known that he would like to be president. There was considerable feeling that it would be good to elect a person from Eastern Europe and that it would not be good to elect an American or other Westerner while in a Soviet bloc country. Bishop Kaldy was elected. Elections to the office were not campaign events. People who wished to nominate you asked if it was all right. I had indicated my willingness, as had Kaldy and several others.

Kaldy spoke much of a Lutheran "theology of diakonia." Some of us saw this as an accommodation to the communist government of Hungary. It certainly worked that way, for Bishop Kaldy was appointed a member of the Hungarian parliament and was given VIP treatment in a variety of ways, including hosting the LWF Assembly. Bishop Kaldy was in the forefront of the LWF leaders in the Soviet bloc countries who believed in open support of their government if the government allowed the churches to continue functioning without a lot of trouble. Kaldy and I were always friends, and while I did not admire him for his stance I could understand it. It is hard to criticize church leaders for accommodating a tyrannical government in order to be allowed mostly normal church life.

During the assembly, however, I took leadership roles in two symbolic actions about which I felt strongly and which elicited Bishop Kaldy's opposition. The first was a visit to the grave of Bishop Kaldy's predecessor, Bishop Ordass, to lay a wreath in memory of his leadership of the church. Bishop Ordass had been an outstanding Lutheran leader, much admired internationally, and an outspoken foe of communism. This earned him the wrath of the communist government of Hungary, and he spent his last few years under house arrest. Ordass represented opposition to communism; Kaldy represented accommodation to communism. Most of the Hungarian Lutherans with whom I became best acquainted liked and admired Ordass but saw no alternative to their church accommodating to the country's rulers, thus agreeing with Kaldy and supporting him. I think Ordass' example most noteworthy. After initial opposition, Kaldy led the graveside service honoring Ordass.

The second action was to call for a memorial service for Raoul Wallenberg, the Swedish diplomat who was famed for saving thousands of Hungarian Jews during the Nazi era and who had then disappeared as a prisoner of the Russian Army. As a way of responding to Wallenberg's world-wide acclaim, the city of Budapest had named a street after him. The street is only one block long and in a little-traveled part of the city. A few of us planned to hold the memorial service on that street. We thought that a significant segment of the assembly delegates would attend the service. However, Bishop Kaldy came before the LWF officers and let it be known that the Hungarian government would consider it an offense and asked that the service be cancelled. The service was not a planned part of the assembly program, but Kaldy's bringing the matter to the LWF officers required a response. I did not think it would be useful to create a confrontation and joined in cancelling the public service. Ann and I and two reporters did privately hold a brief service under the Wallenberg street sign.

The LWF officers had a very interesting meeting with Hungarian Prime Minister Janas Kadar. At the meeting Kadar was genial, friendly, never without a cigarette, an all-around hail-fellow well-met. He looked just like a Hollywood version of a Chicago gangster, leather-faced with his nose somewhat bent out of shape. The burden of his rambling forty-minute address to us (in a time that was supposed to be a conversation) was that there was no reason for the state and the churches to have any trouble. It was just a plain and simple matter of quid pro quo. "As long as the church gives me no trouble, I will give the church no trouble." The hooker, of course, is how the church must act in order to avoid giving the state any trouble. The LWF Assembly gave Hungary no trouble and, apart from the Wallenberg affair, the government gave the LWF no trouble. Those of us from the West had a strong sense of the captivity of the church even in a moderate communist state.

What follows illustrates the work done by the LWF and the various roles of the LWF officers. The fact that all LWF meetings included personnel from various countries was a huge boost to the awareness of global oneness in Christ among Lutherans. The LWF departments of Studies, Church Cooperation, World Service, and Communications were active in many countries. Their work differed widely from one country to the next. What follows is only a brief resume of LWF work in various regions of the world.

Eastern Europe

The LWF and WCC did outstanding work in support of the churches in Eastern Europe during the Iron Curtain years. The Iron Curtain ran down the center of one of the biggest concentration of Lutherans in the world. It was a time of suffering and hardship for Lutheran Christians in East Germany, Hungary, Latvia, Estonia, Lithuania, Romania, Poland, Czechoslovakia, Yugoslavia, and Russia. The physical deprivations were bad enough. The constant Soviet pressure to give up the faith made it even worse. Increased awareness of oneness in Christ across any kind of human-made boundaries was one positive that resulted from East-West enmity.

Some very secular priorities in the Soviet-dominated areas made it possible for the Eastern churches to receive many kinds of assistance from Western churches. Soviet Zone Lutherans were always threatened and fearful, frequently felt alone, isolated, deprived, and helpless. LWF churches in the West were able to provide many East Zone Lutherans and others with food and clothing, religious education materials, Bibles, scholarships, funds, personal visitations, family connections, and awareness that common membership in the body of Christ kept Christians from East and West together. A paragraph in my journal is a typical report of LWF activity:

February 1982 in *The Month That Was*

LWF has helped rebuild and reopen 1,000 churches in Eastern Europe; built buildings, supplied books, and assisted with salaries for teachers in seven major Eastern European seminaries—Hungary, Romania, Poland, Estonia, Latvia, East Germany, and Czechoslovakia. Through the lean years it was the grandmothers, taking care of their grandchildren while the parents worked, who nurtured the faith and kept it alive for a new generation. Now, surprisingly, many young people are going to the churches regardless of the cost. There are now many catechists in East Germany. They work quietly, avoiding attention, but they are there.

As an LWF officer I had opportunities to address East European government officials, especially the ministers for church affairs, on behalf of the Eastern European Lutheran churches. The state ministers for church affairs were of great importance, because the Soviet leaders considered that the churches "belonged" to the state and always tried to make sure the church members knew it. Most church leaders were constantly involved in efforts to maintain separation between church and state. I met with the East Germany minister for church affairs three times, the Hungarian minister twice, the Romanian minister once, the Polish minister twice, and had several meetings with the Soviet minister, including hosting him during his visit to the U.S. In all instances I had been briefed by church leaders as to their concerns before meeting with the state ministers for church affairs. Each time there were lively exchanges, and I would urge freedom to expand the legal limits of church activities. There was no way to know for sure whether the meetings contributed to the relaxation of government restraints. The church leaders in those countries, however, always felt it a victory to have a church leader from the West bring their needs and hopes before the government officials. I could say things that they could not for fear of retribution. That was enough to make me feel the meetings were worthwhile.

A dramatic such meeting was in East Germany at the height of East-West tension. Evangelical youth were publicly agitating for peace and had organized a youth peace movement. Predictably, the state was cracking down on them. In meeting with the East German minister for church affairs I was able to point to the independent youth peace movements in the countries of the West and say how important it would be to have like groups in the East. I remember that Minister Gysi of East Germany lost his cool, slammed his desk, and declared, "Socialism *is* the peace movement."

In 1983 a remarkable series of events occurred around a celebration of Martin Luther's 500th birthday. They were illustrations of the church-state difficulties in East Germany and the way the Christian people worked to keep their churches from being vassals of the state. The government had asked the churches to have a series of joint church-state celebratory events during a week long celebration of Martin Luther's

500th birthday. The churches refused joint celebration of Luther's birthday and indicated that there would be a series of church events with LWF international guests. The government responded by staging Luther events on its own. A show of peace was made when the government invited the church leaders to an official state celebration at the Berlin Opera House and the churches responded by inviting government leaders to a service of celebration at the St. Thomas Church in Leipzig.

East Germany President Honecker hosted the event at the Opera House. There were speeches declaring that Luther was the grandfather of the socialist regime in the Democratic Deutsche Republic (DDR), a marvelous concert by the Berlin Philharmonic with Mendelssohn's "Reformation Symphony" the highlight, and a lavish reception with President Honecker and his cabinet as hosts.

Much more impressive was the service at St. Thomas Church in Leipzig, the church where J.S. Bach served most of his productive years. The contrast of church and state was striking. Four of us church representatives who spoke were seated on one side of the chancel with a group of East German church leaders. Fifteen feet across, facing us, were members of the East German government cabinet. It was an incredibly emotional moment. The packed church roared the opening hymn, "Come Holy Spirit, Enter In." The government cabinet members stood silent, lips pursed. It was a moment of challenge. It happened a second time with the singing of "A Mighty Fortress Is Our God." Cardinal Willebrands, Vatican secretary for Christian unity, spoke first. Next was Archbishop of Canterbury Runcie. Next was Metropolitan Philaret of the Russian Orthodox Church. I spoke for the Lutherans at the request of LWF President Kibira whose illness kept him home in Tanzania. The whole event was an exhilarating experience, but with overtones of sadness.

When the service ended about thirty young people sat in the balcony and lit candles as a sign they were members of the outlawed peace movement. The police were there quickly and hustled them off. A group of German Lutheran bishops followed, and we were informed next morning that they were successful in having the young people released. In retrospect I think the DDR officials were already despairing of their efforts to win the hearts of their citizens.

Later, under the headings of Cold War and nuclear disarmament, I will have much more to say about the LWF in Eastern Europe.

Africa

In dollar terms the LWF work in Africa probably exceeded expenditures in Eastern Europe. Wonderful projects were undertaken in many African settings. A remarkable Radio Voice of the Gospel, based in Addis Ababa, Ethiopia, regularly aired programs in numerous African countries until confiscated by the Ethiopian communist government. The development of schools—elementary, secondary, and seminary—and medical centers occurred alongside missionary activities. The LWF relief and development arm, Lutheran World Service (LWS), brought basic necessities of life to thousands of communities.

Wells were drilled in many parts of Africa to provide the first fresh, clean water that many of the communities had ever seen. Agricultural assistance brought better strains of seeds and livestock, and introduced fertilizers and other ways of improving the land. Scholarships were provided for large numbers of outstanding students, enabling them to bring to their home countries greatly expanded knowledge in many disciplines. Throughout Africa, and especially in South Africa and Namibia, LWF assisted the indigenous peoples in battling racism and the lingering effects of colonialism.

Refugee assistance and resettlement was a massive task in Africa and elsewhere. I reported to the ALC constituency on such activities as often as possible. Following is from a report I made in 1973.

During 1973 LWF-LWS has supported the following efforts:

1. Close to 20,000 Jehovah's Witnesses were expelled from Malawi. LWF assisted them as they resettled in Zambia.

2. Over 30,000 Burundi refugees who found asylum in Tanzania have been assisted. Of seven camps established by LWF, five have now been totally turned over to the Tanzanian government.

3. The Ugandans resettled in the U.S. were initially helped by LWS, then in the U.S. by LIRS; 319 resettled in the U.S. under LIRS-arranged sponsorships.

4. Cooch Behar Refugee Service helped refugees from what was East Pakistan. Refugee camps were built, and LWF directly cared for 150,000 refugees.

5. Rangpur/Dinajpur Rehab Service helped huge numbers—unable to count how many—build new communities in Bangladesh.

Asia, Asia-Minor

In some Asian settings LWF-LWS did the sort of relief and development work that was done in Africa. That was true in India, Bangladesh, Papua New Guinea, and among refugee populations in various countries, including Vietnam, Laos, and Cambodia. Education was always a high priority along with food, clothing, medical, and refugee services.

LWF work in Palestine-Israel was aimed at providing services for poor Palestinian Arabs in Jerusalem and the West Bank and for several hundred thousand Palestinians in refugee camps. There was also support for a handful of small indigenous Lutheran congregations. The Augusta Victoria Lutheran Hospital was for many years the only hospital facility available to the Palestinian Arab population. Frequent negotiations with the Israeli government were necessary to assure continuance of the hospital. An LWS job training program for the blind was a thrill to behold.

A July 1980 report in my journal, *The Month That Was*, is another evidence of the breadth and depth of service provided by LWF-LWS.

> Last year LWS expended $48 million in assistance besides providing avenues for great amounts of government aid. The thanks of delegates from all over the world would stir your hearts. Some of the projects reported include the repatriation of 50,000 exiles from Zimbabwe; refugee camps in Angola for Namibian people fleeing the devastation in Ovamboland; emergency food aid in Kampuchea; plans for a new hospital serving West Bank Arabs in Jerusalem; a food program over several months that maintained life for 90,000 people in Northern Bangladesh.

The Americas

The LWF was active in South America but on a much lesser scale than in Africa or Asia. Much work was done through an LWF member church in Brazil, and there was some support for Lutherans in Argentine, Chile, Colombia, Ecuador, Bolivia, and Guiana. These churches also served as avenues for relief and development work. The same was true in Central America. Some support work was provided in El Salvador, Nicaragua, Honduras, and Guatemala. Usually LWF worked with and through indigenous Lutheran churches. There was not much Lutheran presence in Latin America except for Brazil, so the amount of work done was limited.

In North America and Western Europe the Lutheran churches did not need the same kind of support as in other parts of the world. Joint study programs with Lutherans from all over the world were important to U.S. and Canadian Lutherans. Even more, the sense of solidarity with the world's Lutherans, the awareness of the interdependence of fellow believers, the feelings of fellowship, the practical outworkings of our oneness in Christ were blessings to the churches.

LWF Primary Theological Issues, 1973-1990

The ALC was also involved in theological issues through the LWF. The first two issues grew out of the lives of member churches that were struggling in especially harsh circumstances. They sought help from LWF in dealing with vexing problems. The third grew out of the necessity for the LWF to determine how its own study department should do its work. The fourth is a problem that faces Lutherans as they seek to express their ecumenical commitments.

1. Evangelism-Development

The Mekane Yesus Church, a member of the LWF, raised a very difficult question about the use of church funds. Ethiopia was in desperate straits because of poverty and drought. It was also a time when the opportunities for evangelism were extraordinary. The Mekane Yesus Church was training evangelists as fast as they could, but their resources were just too small. Their request for financial help for evangelism met with limited response. But when it came to funds for relief and development, their requests were met speedily and generously. How much value does the church place on its evangelizing as compared to relief and development was the Mekane Yesus question. It is a recurring question that the church debates, decides, or ignores. The question keeps popping up. There was no definitive answer. Fortunately the Mekane Yesus Church has continued to grow at a phenomenal rate.

2. Status Confessionis

The black LWF member churches in South Africa called for the support of the rest of the LWF member churches in their battle against apartheid. The small, white Lutheran church bodies in South Africa, mostly transplanted Germans, were being urged to unite with the black church bodies, but they found it both difficult and complicated to do so. There was widespread suspicion that the white South African Lutherans favored apartheid. The LWF engaged in lengthy theological debate and came up with a proposal that opposition to apartheid was a matter of *status confessionis*, a declaration that Lutherans must stand in opposition to apartheid as a matter of Christian confession. It was as strong a word as the LWF body could give. It was addressed to Lutheran churches in all the countries that were in various ways aiding and abetting the segregated, white, privileged class in South Africa. It was also addressed to the white Lutheran churches in South Africa who were dragging their feet in relations with black Lutheran churches. Through the statement, the LWF declared that it was no less than a call from God to oppose apartheid and, as churches, to stand together in that opposition.

A quote from the January 1984 *The Month That Was* gives my understanding of the term *status confessionis*.

> It is difficult in that there is no nice, clear, simple, historical definition for the phrase. My best understanding at the moment is that the church may declare a special state of confession where the witness of the church is grossly undercut by a societal accepted doctrine and practice. It is to be distinguished from the continuing confession, with its ethical implications that is always a part of the life and witness of the church. The Nazi claims and the apartheid practice are the two contemporary issues requiring the special call for *status confessionis*. Fear was expressed that the term's use would proliferate to the point of meaninglessness.

In the course of the LWF debate it was pointed out that the LWF is not a church and hence not in a position to make such a declaration. Virtually all of us delegates were in no mood to argue whether or not it was technically correct. We overwhelmingly voted for it and sent it to the member churches for their adoption. The ALC adopted it without dissent and declared the ALC to be in a *status confessionis* with regard to apartheid.

3. Traditional Theology or Action-Reflection

The LWF Studies Department was torn by what many saw as a struggle between the old and the new. The new way to do theology was to engage in action for peace or against poverty, etc., and then reflect on how that experience informs theology. Others framed the struggle quite differently. They saw it as necessary to do contemporary theological work in such a way that it would provide guidance for Christian action in the world. In the one, the theology came first. In the other, the action came first. It is one of the enduring questions that never reaches complete resolution. The LWF battle was hard, however, because it was traditional for Lutheran theology to provide guidance for the action. The LWF ultimately stayed with the traditional, an action I supported

4. Ecclesial Density—LWF

A great deal of debate over several years focused on whether the LWF should be referred to as a "Lutheran communion" or as a federation of independent churches. Those wishing for the LWF to be called a communion argued that the term "federation" did not adequately describe the nature of the church as the communion of saints. They felt that greater ecclesial density accompanies the words "Lutheran communion." On the other side was the argument that communion among the LWF member churches already exists and that referring to the LWF as a federation simply and accurately described the organizational reality of the LWF. I remember President Schiotz at Evian saying that it is taken for granted that LWF member churches are in altar and pulpit fellowship with each other. Underlying the debate is the question of juridical authority. Is there, or should there be, a "higher" level of church that has some measure of ecclesial authority over the LWF member churches? The two LWF general secretaries with whom I served, Andre Appel and Carl Mau, suggested that the LWF general secretary should be titled "bishop." They felt that their position would be enhanced in necessary dealings with the pope and other church leaders if their role was seen as that of a bishop. I saw both the "communion" and "bishop" suggestions as moves to strengthen the authority of the LWF. I thought it important that the LWF be seen as a serving center rather than as a power center. I thought the negatives outweighed the gains in the proposals to strengthen LWF ecclesial density, and hence I opposed them.

The matter of ecclesial density has wide-ranging implications, and I expect it will remain an issue indefinitely.

CHAPTER ELEVEN

GLOBAL ECUMENICAL RELATIONS—WCC

WCC Governance

The WCC operated similarly to the LWF only with a broader constituency. Financial support for member churches in strained circumstances was always high on the agenda as was a massive Church World Service relief and development program in dozens of countries.

When I first took office I asked Dr. Warren Quanbeck, a theological professor and former teacher of mine, to represent the ALC on the WCC Central Committee. He had been one of a few Protestants invited to be an observer and participant at Vatican II. I felt certain he would make an excellent theological contribution to the WCC. Unfortunately death claimed him after only a few years of WCC service. The WCC general secretary, Phillip Potter, made a strong personal plea that I represent the ALC, and he had a page full of reasons why it was important for me to do so. They were convincing, and I agreed to serve on the Central Committee. Two years later I was elected to the much smaller and more influential executive committee.

While the governance responsibilities with the WCC were similar to those in the LWF, the actual participation was quite different. The executive committee brought together persons from widely differing church and theological backgrounds. Members included a militant Russian Orthodox archbishop, a very aggressive and theologically liberal free church London newspaper reporter, a Scotch Presbyterian school teacher, an angry pentecostalist from Zaire, a left-wing bishop from the Mar Thoma Church in India, a very bright and delightful laywoman from one of the Caribbean Islands, an outstanding laywoman from the Coptic Church in Egypt, a strong Lutheran bishop from East Germany, and a feisty woman church leader from the United Church of Canada.

The following quotation from my journal of March 9, 1981, gives a feel for the main tasks undertaken by the WCC and their difficulties:

The breadth of need and the limits of finance are the overwhelming realities that press on both WCC and LWF executive committees. Delegate after delegate outlines the critical needs of a particular church and seeks WCC help. Just the question of scholarships can trigger a chorus of concern with a welter of different needs, all requiring different processes. The role of women evokes a wide range of concern. The Orthodox lament is that all WCC work in the women's area is done by women who have been chosen precisely because they are feminists. The women produce predictable results, and the Orthodox get predictably angry. In spite of all the difficulties coming from so many sources, there is a remarkable convergence of concern and action in some areas. There is, for instance, great applause for programs relating to renewal in congregational life. There are a great many churches all around the world that do not have a Division for Life and Mission in the Congregation. They are dependent on special services that come from WCC or LWF or other confessional groups. So a church of a few thousand or several million in Zambia, or in South Korea, or in Indonesia, looks to Geneva for assistance. The small WCC staff, facing language barriers, debate on educational policy and theological niceties, is understandably harried and seeking sympathy. The surprising and encouraging thing is that they are able to do enough to receive effusive thanks from many directions.

The WCC was aggressively engaged in representing the world's poor and oppressed especially by supporting various liberation movements. That created a good deal of controversy and criticism. The heaviest criticism was leveled at the WCC Program to Combat Racism through which the WCC provided funds for humane purposes through the liberation movements. It was impossible to definitely ascertain that the funds were always used for the intended purposes, so critics accused the WCC of providing funds for rebel military groups. The assumption of critics was that liberation movements were ipso facto communist movements. The Cold War was at its peak and the Soviets were trying to gain influence in African countries, so there were points to be made about Soviet influence. However, the WCC member churches in Africa were uniformly supportive of those liberation movements which they saw as movements for independence and justice. Also the WCC presumed that the victims of violence should receive such care as the WCC could provide regardless of their politics. In most instances there was assurance that the funds provided were used for humanitarian purposes. To placate the critics in various countries, the Program to Combat Racism used only funds from churches that designated them for that purpose. That helped those who were from WCC member churches who had a significant number of members critical of the WCC and its Program to Combat Racism.

The WCC also took a good deal of criticism for failure to protest against the Soviet countries in a way comparable to the frequent criticism of the U.S. and the West. This issue was debated vigorously by those of us in leadership positions. I met only one WCC representative who actually supported Soviet communism, but many WCC delegates and staff felt the WCC should avoid protesting for the sake of the well-being of the churches in those countries. It was hard to ignore the pleas of the Eastern European WCC delegates who would ask that the WCC forego public criticism of Eastern governments in order to protect the churches in the Eastern countries from governmental crackdowns. I was one of those who thought that WCC criticism could not be consistently one-sided. I joined others in efforts, sometimes effective, to keep the WCC at least somewhat even-handed in addressing faults of East and West.

The various WCC departments did outstanding work in support of the churches in the most impoverished countries. Its Church World Service relief and development agency worked parallel to Lutheran World Service. Combining the two agencies was often considered, however each group provided access to some countries where the other was not welcome. That, plus the fact that both groups were large enough to carry out global programs, and the two units worked in tandem wherever it was useful, meant that there was no good reason to change. I was very impressed at the way the various church relief agencies coordinated their activities.

The ALC made an especially important contribution to the fight against poverty through a fledgling WCC organization called the Ecumenical Cooperative Development Cooperative Society (EDCS). The society provided loans to small, productive, potentially cost-effective businesses. It expected repayment and had an excellent track record in that regard. The key was in making small loans to individuals and groups who had no collateral. I believe this was the first of such programs, the success of which has been instrumental in inspiring other organizations and governments to start similar programs in various countries. After becoming acquainted with ECDS, I recommended that the ALC make a major contribution. The ALC's $250,000 was by far the largest single grant, and it greatly expanded the number of loans that could be made. It also opened the door for other major church bodies to make sizable grants. The ALC's George Schultz had played a seminal role in starting the program, became a board member, and was a major leader for several years. His successor, David Rokke, continued the good work. Thousands of loans have been made, and most of the small businesses have prospered enough to repay their loans and provide employment for thousands of people. It is one of those relatively small things that breathes life into dysfunctional societies and encourages other changes.

Special Assignments

I had several special assignments while serving on the WCC executive committee. In 1982 Poland was under martial law as protests against the government increased. There were several small Protestant churches and a larger Orthodox church that formed an ecumenical council in this predominantly Roman Catholic country. The Polish ecumenical council requested a visitation from the WCC in order to remind their people and the government that these churches were linked with a broad global network of churches. I was one of a three-person team that made the visitation. We met with Poland's President Jaroslav Jaruzelski and Archbishop Glemp, primate of Poland's Roman Catholic Church. President Jaruzelski gave us long lecture on the need for Poland to invoke martial law in order to stop the unrest caused by Lech Walesa and the Solidarity movement. While in Poland we met with church councils, congregations, and other Polish authorities, as well as with the ecumenical council. I also had the opportunity to meet with the Polish Lutheran Church Council and also with congregants of two Lutheran congregations separated by several hundred miles. We witnessed to the depth of friendship and support the Polish church bodies had with other churches throughout the world. It was a useful visit, another peace-seeking link between West and East.

An interesting experience grew out of the Polish visit. The next time I was in Geneva, I received a call at the LWF offices from a man who identified himself as the "third secretary" at the Polish embassy. He invited me to lunch to talk about our visit to Poland. That is, indeed, what we talked about. He asked about various aspects of the trip. It gradually became apparent that he was on a fishing expedition. He wanted something from me, was looking for some way to "use" me, but I never discovered if he had something particular in mind. I do not think he was a third secretary, rather an intelligence agent. I think it highly likely he sought to recruit me, at least to create an opportunity for me to volunteer services for Poland and/or the Soviet Union.

On another occasion I served on the search committee for a new WCC general secretary. There were two very lively meetings with much discussion about the WCC's future direction as well as reviewing the credentials of nominees. In a very closely contested vote the committee nominated Emilio Castro of Uruguay, who was elected and served for the ensuing seven years. Castro was the first Latin to serve as secretary.

A third special assignment came during the WCC Assembly in Vancouver, British Colombia. Moderator Gatu of the Kenya Presbyterian Church and I were asked to attend a meeting of the Native Americans imprisoned at the British Colombia penitentiary in order to receive a gift from them to the WCC. It was a strange assignment, but it proved to be a very moving experience. The group of prisoners had worked for several months to carve and paint a forty-foot totem pole that they gave to the WCC. The pole was transported to Geneva where it since has stood at the front of the WCC headquarters building. It is an intricately carved and painted piece. The presentation was especially moving because of two speeches. The Native American who made the presentation spoke of the desire of the prisoners to identify with the WCC. He spoke movingly of the plight of the Canadian and Alaskan Native Americans and thanked the prison authorities for the permission to create the totem pole. Even more moving was the WCC reception speech given by President Gatu. He told of his own years as a rebellious youth, of his criminal record, of his imprisonment in Kenya. Then he gave a moving testimony to the power and love of Christ, and the strength of the global communion of saints. He concluded by assuring the Native Americans that the totem pole would be a symbol of the unity between widely differing peoples and countries.

WCC Theological Issues

Ecclesial Density—WCC

Following a 1980 executive committee meeting of the World Council of Churches, I wrote an informal *The Month That Was* letter that was sent to a broad leadership of the American Lutheran Church. It contained the following paragraph.

> A recurring theme, "the ecclesial character of the World Council of Churches," was again prominent in the deliberations. Phillip Potter, a very strong executive secretary of the WCC, announced this would be a major thrust of his report to the assembly. The question is whether the council is an agency of the churches, an association of independent churches that can take or leave what the majority votes, or whether it has a churchly, an ecclesial, character of its own. As I mentioned previously, this question has also been before the Lutheran World Federation. It will be with us continually, I suspect.

Clearly Phillip Potter sought a strengthened ecclesial role for the WCC. It was not simply a matter of personal aggrandizement. It was a matter of governance. He sought a more determinative WCC voice in the lives of the far-flung churches that made up the WCC membership. The WCC was created to enable the churches to show their unity in addressing global well-being. Outstanding Christians from all over the globe were gathered to provide the best possible information, decisions were made, and Potter felt strongly that WCC should see those decisions as mandatory in the churches' lives. Instead the executive secretary had the difficult task of rallying the member churches to support WCC decisions made by representatives from the churches. He had to play a key role in encouraging the churches to provide adequate financial and personnel support and at the same time seek to be a prophetic Christian voice in a conflicted and often violent world. The job was not easy.

I supported efforts to deepen the sense of communion among the churches of both LWF and WCC. However, I opposed any effort to make the groups stronger legislative bodies. I believed the "communion" of LWF and WCC member churches was real and apparent and was steadily being strengthened as global communications and joint activities were strengthened. I understood the frustrations of LWF and WCC staff at the slow and uncertain acceptance of decisions made by those groups. However, I also believed that it was necessary to oppose efforts to make the LWF and WCC the highest legislative bodies in the lives of the churches. The move for greater ecclesial density, to my mind, was also an effort to strengthen the authoritative role of those bodies. I thought it important that such bodies remain primarily service agencies of local congregations through their church bodies and not power centers that could determine the stances of the churches.

It is my contention that the WCC and LWF are not hierarchal governing bodies. Their jurisdiction, their decisions, ought not to be determinative but persuasive. If church bodies and their congregations are not persuaded on a given issue, they should be free to dissent and voice their opposition to the issue. Ultimately the councils are created by local congregations through church bodies the congregations have formed. It is important that congregations be able to extend their ministries through associations with other congregations. Church bodies and councils *are* agencies of the congregations. It is a common sense matter for the congregation that believes it is called to make disciples of and serve the entire world. The WCC and LWF should be subject to the will of the church bodies that have been the instruments in creating them. The clusters of congregations called church bodies should be able to take or leave what the WCC or LWF votes. What is the point of telling any group of member congregations that they are subject to the vote of a higher body and are therefore incapable of making their own decisions?

Of course there is an ecclesial character to these large international bodies. They are manifestations of the unity of Christ's church, and they are the way congregations do important extended services. They are not intended to be governing agencies that carry ever-increasing authority as breadth of membership increases. The church is not a "top down" corporate operation where the "higher" unit is God's instrument that requires concurrence from the "lesser" church bodies and congregations.

There was always a disjunction among WCC churches as to the nature of WCC unity as it presently exists and what its future unity goals should be. Some WCC delegates tilted toward an ultimate goal of a single global church organization. To them, the WCC is a step on the way. Some made it clear that an even wider unity, including those outside the Christian faith, was their goal. Others thought the WCC good as it was; it should look to expand WCC membership while concentrating on doing the mission of the church and not worrying about church organization. I supported the view that the WCC is now a conciliar fellowship and should seek broader participation of churches while concentrating on the evangelical and service sectors of discipleship. The thought is that the church will always exist in different forms and have various theological bases and ethnic and linguistic identities, but will involve mutual recognition of Christian faith and willingness to do whatever joint activity makes sense.

In retrospect it appears to me that the issue of ecclesial density underlay, at least in part, my support for unity options short of U.S. Lutheran merger, support for reconciled diversity in the LWF, and support for conciliar fellowship in the WCC.

Support for Political Ideologies

Even with agreement that the churches have a social responsibility to address issues of injustice, there remained wide differences regarding support to strong "leftist" or "rightist" regimes. The greatest conflict of conviction occurred around the WCC Program to Combat Racism. Most often there was a socialist political ideology undergirding these efforts. While the majority of WCC delegates supported revolutionary efforts designed to aid the poor, there was always some uncertainty as to whether the WCC support alleviated injustice or supported socialist goals. My sense was that most delegates understood their Christian responsibility to support those in great need and yet to oppose the frequent tyranny of socialist states. The issue was troublesome throughout my years with the WCC.

International Lutheran-Roman Catholic Relations

At the international level, the public actions of Roman Catholic and Lutheran leaders reflected the positive developments in local ecumenicity. A Roman Catholic representative from the Vatican Secretariat for Christian Unity always participated at LWF executive committee meetings, and Lutheran leaders had frequent meetings with Roman Catholic counterparts.

At one point, crucial change took place in the official theological discussions between Roman Catholics and Lutherans. The discussions concentrated on the doctrinal similarities instead of focusing on the differences—a great change from previous generations. At the 1983 celebration of Martin Luther's birth, Roman Catholic representatives took part in most of the public activities. A great Lutheran gathering in the historic city of Worms was addressed by the present Pope Benedict, who was then Cardinal Ratzinger of Munich. The LWF officers were invited to participate in the installation of Pope John Paul I, and three of us were able to attend. We were treated royally and had productive meetings with the Roman Catholic Secretary for Christian Unity, Cardinal Willebrands. The cardinal pointed out to us how the language of the popes had changed when speaking of the Protestants. In the Reformation era and long thereafter Lutherans and other Protestants were "apostates." Centuries later the Protestants were identified as "separated brethren." Pope John Paul I referred to Protestants as "brothers and sisters in Christ." To me the death of Pope John Paul I was a huge tragedy. I believe he was ready for much greater ecumenical and social change than his successor.

In 1983 I arranged to meet with Pope John Paul II at the Vatican. I wanted to give him my view of the positive growth in relationships between U.S. Roman Catholics and Lutherans, and to see if we could facilitate joint worship services. The conversation was friendly and wide-ranging. He agreed that Roman Catholic and Lutheran representatives should develop a worship service for use at Lutheran-Roman Catholic joint services. Such a service was developed and was first used at a joint meeting of Roman Catholic and Lutheran bishops. One of the Roman Catholic bishops preached and I presided at the service at Reformation Lutheran Church in Washington, D.C.

The international Lutheran-Roman Catholic dialogue reflected and increased the mutual positive agreements between the two groups. Much common ground was found in areas that previously were only contentious. Even justification by faith, so central a dividing point, allowed for more agreement than ever before acknowledged. Again I emphasize that the great change that has taken place is in the attitudes of Roman Catholics and Lutherans toward each other. That is at the heart of the new readiness to work on confessional issues. The doctrinal differences between Rome and the Reformation churches remain deep and broad and will remain so for the foreseeable future. It is the attitude that has changed, and that made possible all sorts of new initiatives. Now there is wide acknowledgment that Lutherans and Roman Catholics are one in Christ, even as they remain critical of each other's formulation of the faith. I cannot foresee the day when Roman Catholics and Lutherans find theological agreement, but I am deeply hopeful that the popular acceptance of each other by laity and clergy will endure.

The outstanding Roman Catholic and Lutheran World Relief agencies have been close working partners in various parts of the world. Agricultural pursuits, famine relief, and refugee resettlement are illustrative of areas where cooperation has been the byword. It has been an ecumenical joy to move beyond old enmities to a shared witness to the lordship of Christ.

Relations with Orthodox Churches

I think it safe to say that there was little consciousness among the vast majority of ALC members that there were such Christian groups as the Orthodox churches. Yet their history dates back to apostolic days, and they are the dominant Christian churches in most of Eastern Europe. Most U.S. Orthodox members are still members of ethnic language groups. Greeks, Russians, Serbs, Bulgarians, Armenians, Ukrainians, Syrians, Egyptian Copts, and others have maintained their native languages in their churches and have generally been slow to share an ecumenical outlook. That has not been true, however, on the international scene. The Orthodox churches decided to become members of the World Council of Churches, and that has worked remarkable changes in ecumenical life. Worshipping and working together in the WCC has necessitated a new level of acquaintance among Orthodox and Protestant Christians, heightening awareness of a unity in Christ that transcends differences. Illustrative is a quote from my journal of March 9, 1981:

> It is a new and exciting development to have Orthodox lay persons serving as WCC staff. Marie Aasaad, Egyptian Coptic, is a new deputy general secretary, and she is a clipper. The same is true of Todor Sabev, a Bulgarian Orthodox lay leader. Both are articulate and excellent at dialogue. The various patriarchs and metropolitans who serve on elected bodies are quite different. They make long, un-understandable speeches and give audible evidence as to why there is great emphasis on the "mystery" of the faith in Orthodox circles. Also, they have a way of finishing their speeches with an assertion that in its finality does not call for a re-

sponse. Yet there is remarkable affection between the lay and hierarchical members of the Orthodox, and wonderful friendships developed between Orthodox and Protestant members of the World Council.

Lutherans and Orthodox became much more aware of each other during the last half of the twentieth century. Some of it had to do with the similar trials in dealing with hardships imposed by communist governments. Also Lutheran and Orthodox geographic areas of strength abut each other. Sizeable minority churches exist in countries where one group or the other dominates. Finnish Lutherans have a significant presence in the Orthodox Leningrad area of Russia, and the Russian Orthodox a similar minority position in Finland. A well-organized group of German Lutherans existed as a small minority in Orthodox Russia for centuries. Scattered throughout Russia during the Stalin era thousands of Lutherans continued to sustain congregational life even in remote Siberia. There is a large though dwindling Lutheran constituency in Romania. Increased acquaintance between Lutherans and Orthodox has resulted in increased awareness of shared central Christian commitments in spite of very different theologies and liturgical life. During my years working with WCC, the ecumenical activity between the LWF and Eastern Orthodox increased dramatically.

Through WCC service I became close with the Orthodox. It started with my service on the WCC executive committee. Then Archbishop, now Metropolitan Kirill was also a member. Another prominent Russian Orthodox churchman, Proto-priest Borovoy, was the permanent Orthodox representative to the WCC and attended most of the meetings. We discovered we held similar theological views about the WCC's international roles and theological seriousness.

An illustration of similar views occurred early in my service on the WCC executive committee. While I was positive about most WCC programs, I kept insisting that the WCC was short-changing its commitment to world missionary centrality. This engaged me in a running debate at executive committee meetings with General Secretary Phillip Potter, who insisted the missionary responsibility was being handled by the individual churches and that those churches looked to the WCC to serve the causes of mercy and justice. I argued that theologically it was both wrong and unwise to regularize such a division of duties. I recognized that a number of countries had prohibited Christian missionary activity and only allowed Christian social ministries. Nevertheless I argued that from the Christian side there could not be an international church agency that divorced itself from its missionary calling. (As an aside: Former general secretary and father of the WCC, Visser 't Hooft, twice caught me after meetings to encourage me to keep saying my piece.)

This point of view resonated with the Orthodox. Subsequently I was appointed co-chair of a Russian Orthodox-sponsored global peace conference, was awarded the Georgia Orthodox Church medal of St. George during a visit with Metropolitan David in Sukhumi, Georgia, and was a guest for Russian Orthodox Christmas with Metropolitan Philaret in Minsk. Because the Patriarch Pimen was aged and quite inactive, I thought it apparent that Metropolitan Philaret was the most looked-to leader of the Russian Orthodox Church. I found a whole cadre of Russian Orthodox Church leaders who are theologically astute and outgoing in friendship.

During the time spent in Russia I concluded that, after decades of open persecution of the Russian Orthodox Church, the Soviet government was now attempting to make the church an ally rather than an enemy. The government needed the loyalty of its own people and had come to recognize that great loyalty to the Russian Orthodox Church continued to exist. Life had been so difficult for Christians for so many years that even a modest shift in government attitude was both welcome and significant. During the 1980s various restrictions on Orthodox life were lifted. It became easier for Orthodox leaders to attend meetings abroad. There was greater freedom for the faithful to gather in churches. There was a distinct let-up in government attempts to eradicate religious belief. I remember meeting in 1983 with the rector of the primary Orthodox seminary in Zagorsk; he told me that they were much encouraged because "many intellectuals and young people were coming to them by night." That would not have been possible in earlier years. Then Archbishop Kirill of Smolensk told how his local congregations had been forbidden for decades to have an annual Christian parade through town. Suddenly permission was given. Kirill told how the communist mayor of the city rushed out to ask if he could ride with the archbishop. The parade included so many people that the mayor wanted to show his support for the event.

A shift in attitude was implied when the Soviet minister for religious affairs and other government officials came to some events sponsored by the church. It seemed increasingly clear to me that the government was attempting to win the church's support rather than focusing on destroying it. This was borne out to me when I became quite well acquainted with the Soviet Minister of Church Affairs Kharkov through meetings in Moscow. He went out of his way to be friendly. Later I hosted Kharkov when he visited Minneapolis during a trip to the U.S., even taking him for a first-hand look at the Billy Graham operation. The Russian government was much concerned about the aggressive and apparently successful Russian evangelistic campaign of Graham-style Baptists. I attended two or three Orthodox Church-sponsored receptions in Moscow at which high level Soviet officials, outstanding university professors, and other communist elite were present. I thought it worth the possibility of being seen as a dupe in order to establish ties with the Russian Orthodox faithful. Eighty-five percent of the Russian Orthodox priests had been sent to gulags during the worst years of oppression, and most of them never returned. It was apparent that, even with improved conditions, the Orthodox faithful whom I came to know were consciously walking on eggshells. I figured that any way Eastern and Western Christians could be together was valuable in itself and an important link in expressing cross-cultural commonality. I still think so.

I hope the release of Soviet archives will include cabinet level records of Soviet leaders' discussions on what to do about the churches. The Lenin and Stalin years were clear in their intent to hasten the end of Christian faith and churches. They realized that the church was the only nationwide non-governmental organization that could possibly register meaningful opposition to the state. It would be fascinating to know why the regime did not purge the nation of Christians as they had purged the nation of recalcitrant peasant farmers. The Soviet government cruelly persecuted Christians, but they stopped short of driving the church completely underground. I think there will be disclosures about the thinking and workings of the Soviet government for decades to come.

CHAPTER 12

THE CHURCH IN THE PUBLIC SQUARE

Meetings with U.S. Government Leaders

President Carter

In 1977 I was invited to a meeting with President Carter at Camp David. It was during a difficult energy crisis, not a happy time for the American people. The president felt there was a general lassitude among Americans and was looking for ways to inspire the U.S. people to look on the difficulties as challenges to overcome and not just trials to be suffered. He had several such meetings with about a dozen participants each time. Our group was primarily religious leaders with one prominent university professor, Robert Bellah of the University of California, who had written an excellent book on the American spirit entitled *Habits of the Heart.* We spent several hours with President and Mrs. Carter. I thought our best suggestions came in asking for straight talk, telling the truth about difficulties with no sugar coating, indicating some ways ordinary people could help, and then calling the American people to the tasks necessary. We pledged ourselves to work to enlist the church's people in the tasks. I think I received the invitation to Camp David because of outspoken support for human rights initiatives, a centerpiece in Carter's program. Or then again, it might have been because of my long-time friendship with Vice President Mondale. It was probably both.

Congressional Leaders

Several U.S. Protestant church leaders met at least twice a year with members of the U.S. Congress. Usually a particular subject was chosen so Congress members with that particular responsibility could be involved. Most often government financing was involved because of the church leaders' efforts to lessen the military budget and increase support for such concerns as equal educational opportunities, health care, food stamps, refugee resettlement, and other forms of aid to the world's poor. The understanding was that the conversations would be two-way, that is, that the members of Congress were not only to listen to the church leaders but also to register their concerns with the church leaders. The meetings were very helpful. To illustrate I cite a meeting in which Congressman Andrew Young of Georgia was a participant. Church leaders were arguing that a military budget cut could be made by reducing the endless increase in nuclear weapons. Andrew Young responded by saying that he would gladly support such reduction in military spending if he could be assured the savings would be used for vocational training for young African-American males. Currently, he said, the military was the only large-scale vocational training available to young African-American people. It was the kind of attention-capturing insight that made us church leaders a little better equipped to deal sensibly with important public issues. Congress people's readiness to dialogue with us was encouraging and helpful. Such luminaries as soon-to-be U.S. President Gerald Ford, Senators Humphrey, Simon, Kennedy, and Hatfield were among the frequent participants.

For Peace, Do Justice

Peacemaking should always be a part of a person's life and work. Whenever people deal with people there is either a positive, peaceful result or a negative, contentious result. Peacemaking is not an exact science. Virtually everybody is in favor of peace. Yet wars flourish, enmity trumps friendship, and the human penchant to seek solutions through violence continues unabated. Peacemaking does not have a standard table of duties. Individuals, churches, and nations have to identify areas of conflict and then creatively seek for ways to help solve conflicts peaceably. History shows how strong is the temptation to turn to violence for solutions.

The church's first peacemaking responsibility is evangelism, the preaching of the gospel of Christ. That is the way people are brought to faith in Christ and peace with God and themselves. However, God does not summon believers to personal inner peace only. Followers of Christ are to positively influence associations between families, clans, tribes, castes, races, religious groups, and nations. Believers are called to battle for justice and peace in every area of life. Working for peace with justice is integral to the church's total witness. Lutherans have a special theological underpinning with Luther's doctrine of two kingdoms.

I came into office with the conviction Lutherans had not adequately expressed the doing of justice as necessary for peace to prevail. Lutherans were strong in doing evangelism through the preaching of the gospel and in doing works of mercy, and they understood about being just and fair in their personal dealings. As a generalization, however, Lutherans had not been strong in concern for justice in matters of public policy. Public policy was secular, hence thought out of the church's purview.

I brought experience from community organizing, civil rights activity, peace movements, and other social efforts wherein the church's motivation for action was public justice as well as mercy. Just like the prophets of old, contemporary Christians have the responsibility to both urge support for legitimate governments and level criticism against social injustice, especially when the needs of the poor and oppressed are ignored. My first ALC convention sermon was entitled "Jesus, Justice, and Joy," and those words continued to guide me throughout my years in office. Support for public policies that are just and criticism of injustice now has become a more generally accepted peacemaking responsibility for American Lutherans. I believe my support for justice and peace played a part in bringing that about.

An illustration of my speeches on justice comes from my ALC greeting to the LCMS convention in Anaheim, California, in July 1975:

> We intend to be devoted to doing justice. God's Word calls us to be diligent in helping create a just human society where half the people do not go to bed hungry tonight and where half the people do not have to live under tyranny. God calls us in the churches to keep battling the demon of racism no matter how weary of the battle the rest of the society becomes. God calls us to hear the cry of all oppressed people and help free all from hunger, poverty, and tyranny as well as from sin, death, and the power of the devil. Lutherans have been justifiably accused of sitting quietly by while injustice occurs unchallenged. We hear God's Word that calls us to "do justice." We intend to plug away at it. That is where we are headed. We ask you to join us.

The ALC, LWF, and WCC conventions took actions that called on the membership to become personal peacemakers. Those conventions also called upon the nations to undertake efforts to end racism, the Cold War, nuclear proliferation, and environmental disaster. The intent was always to cause thinking and action by the ALC constituency and to influence policy makers. My responsibility was to give voice to the church's statements and in my own life to serve the causes of justice and peace. The office of president provided many unique opportunities to do so.

I urged peace among the nations of the world in a variety of ways. Efforts to affect the globe-threatening stand-off between the superpowers, the U.S. and the Soviet Union, will be addressed later under the titles, Cold War and Nuclear Disarmament. Speeches and written articles were directed especially to the ALC constituency. There were participations in a variety of national and international peace gatherings. There were personal representations to members of the U.S. administration and Congress. Of special significance were many meetings with church and government representatives on both sides of the Iron Curtain. To use contemporary slang, I was engaged in a great deal of jaw-boning and cheerleading in behalf of justice and peace.

It is true that social justice causes can dominate the church's agenda in a way that confuses and diminishes the priority of gospel proclamation. It is impossible to embrace a critical social cause without becoming passionate about it. Then there comes a temptation to see the Christian faith through the prism of a cause rather than the other way around. Clarity about God's two kingdoms is essential—the one centered in the gospel and the other centered in the law, the one served by the church and the other by the state. The ALC constituency, including me, was very wary of allowing the public square to dominate the church's life. While seeking to fulfill my duties as a church spokesperson for public social causes, I also sought opportunities to preach the gospel in order to keep balance in my own life. Luther said the church is a "mouth house," always having the primary responsibility to speak the gospel. Speaking the gospel and participating in public life should not be in conflict. The gospel deals with the saving presence of God and the public realm with earthly justice. I believe the ALC kept the distinctions clear while witnessing to the fact that they go together.

Justice and Israel

In 1978 U.S. President Jimmy Carter asked me to accompany Vice President Walter Mondale as a member of a delegation representing the U.S. at a thirtieth anniversary celebration of the State of Israel. More important than the celebration was the Vice President's assignment to create momentum for peace between Israel and Egypt. His meetings with

Prime Minister Begin of Israel and President Sadat of Egypt triggered a series of events that resulted in a major turn toward peace between the two leaders and their countries. The thirty of us in the delegation were not directly involved in the negotiations, but we surely came as peacemakers. For three days we met with Israeli cabinet members, media, and people on the streets. Everyone knew we were there to encourage peaceful relations between two countries that had in recent years fought each other in three different wars.

An occasion of high drama for me occurred when President Menachim Begin of Israel hosted Vice President and Mrs. Mondale and the rest of the American delegation at a state dinner in the foyer of the Knesset. The setting was stunning. Three immense tapestries by the artist Marc Chagall provided the backdrop for the head table. One of the extraordinarily colored hangings depicts the creation, another the exodus, and the third King David dancing into Jerusalem. Seated in front of the tapestries were Prime Minister and Mrs. Begin, Vice President and Mrs. Mondale, General and Mrs. Moshe Dayan, and Israeli President and Mrs. Weiszman. The Israeli cabinet and the Amercan delegation were seated at tables facing the tapestries. In retrospect the event becomes even more dramatic, for the meeting proved to be the beginning of a successful peace process between Israel and Egypt.

It is now thirty years later, and the Egypt-Israeli peace accords have held. It is one of the few relatively peaceful contemporary results between Middle East countries. The Middle East and the whole world were given opportunity to see that there can be peaceful results other than one side beating up on the other. Those of us in the delegation came home with a sense of accomplishment and gratitude. But we also came home with the awareness that the Middle East in total remained a seething cauldron of anger and violence. I wrote the following words on the way home.

> It is easy to become pessimistic about the possibilities for peace in the Middle East. The turmoil of competing interests is intense. Historic hatreds run deep. Finding security for a small nation like Israel is a military puzzle. Finding a just solution for the Palestinian Arabs is a tormenting problem. One wonders if the United States can really play peacemaker by providing more and more arms to both sides in the conflict.

Palestinian-Israeli Impasse

On another visit to Israel during the years I was on the Minneapolis School board, I spent several days studying Israeli efforts to provide equal educational opportunities for well-educated youth with European backgrounds and educationally deprived and economically impoverished Jewish youth from Middle Eastern and African countries. Then I spent several days visiting with some of the small number of Arab Lutherans and seeing the LWF work among the Palestinian Arabs.

LWF work with Israel was very limited but impressive. The chief job was to intercede with the Israeli government to avoid confiscation of LWF properties, especially the Augusta Victoria Hospital. In addition to the hospital, the LWF had an outstanding vocational school for the blind, an excellent mobile clinic that visited Arab villages, and a number of village projects for which the LWF provided materials and local residents the labor. When I was with the Palestinians I could identify with the Arab concerns and understand their frustration and feel the injustice of their lot. The Palestinians were driven out of their homes and lands, and they believe themselves victims of grave injustice. And when I was with the Israelis I could understand their deep feeling of need for a Jewish homeland and the history of injustice that had led to the establishment of Israel.

Doing justice is frequently complicated by long histories of injustice. The Israeli-Palestinian impasse is surely an illustration of that fact.

Justice and Anti-Semitism

Lutherans and Jews for many years had various national and international joint committees at work to address anti-Semitism. In the U.S. I appointed an ALC committee to develop a positive statement on Lutheran-Jewish relations. The statement was warmly welcomed by U.S. Jewish leadership. There were numerous official and unofficial conferences between Lutherans and Jews, and I believe they helped to diminish anti-Semitism and strengthen friendships. In 1987 I was invited to address the American Reformed Rabbinical Association. The very prominent Jewish B'nai B'rith Association took note of ALC work by presenting me their Torch of Liberty award.

Throughout the last fifty years Protestant-Jewish relations on a global scale have been on the agenda of both WCC and LWF. Lutherans have publicly declared repentance for their failures to curb the anti-Semitism that has been such a blot on Christian history. Even more importantly, the Lutheran-Jewish meetings have pointed toward creating structures and attitudes that would assure a positive and peaceful future for the two peoples.

Justice and Native Americans

Relations between Native Americans and the rest of U.S. society have never been good. ALC people, like the rest of American society, do not really know how to be peacemakers with a people that has been so decimated and marginalized by the majority society. The ALC did try to help. A National Indian Lutheran Board (NILB) was established to enable ALC Native Americans to address the wider culture and to support efforts seeking justice for Native Americans. There were only a handful of ALC Native American congregations, but a significant number of Native Americans were members of predominantly Caucasian congregations. NILB was formed by Native American Lutherans who came from all over the U.S. and from many different tribal groups. The NILB provided a gathering point for the scattered Native American Lutherans and, through modest ALC annual grants, they were able to support a variety of Native American causes.

Paul Boe was an ALC national staff person who worked extensively with Native American people and through his work came to identify himself with various Native American causes. He was much loved by Indian people and was with a group organized as the American Indian Movement (AIM) when they encamped at Wounded Knee, South Dakota. A standoff with U.S. marshals developed, and Wounded Knee was surrounded by armed marshals. The tension was great for a couple of weeks, and there was much national and international publicity. Paul Boe was the only non-American Indian allowed within the Wounded Knee enclave, and he sought to bring a Christian ministry to the community. Many South Dakotans, including many ALC members, were incensed at the Native Americans. It was especially galling to them that Paul Boe, one of their church's executives, should identify with them.

When the standoff was settled, Paul Boe was arrested for aiding and abetting illegal activity and refusing to testify against the Indian leaders. Paul stood ready to go to jail rather than testify against the Indian leadership. He believed his duty as a Christian pastor would be compromised if he disclosed information about a people who had looked to him as friend and pastor. I stood by him and flew with him to Sioux Falls, South Dakota, where he was to face federal charges. It was a moving moment when we were welcomed at the Sioux Falls airport by a large group of Native Americans, drums beating and the leaders wearing traditional Indian garb. We held a prayer service at a local church and prepared to go en masse to the courthouse when a message was received announcing that the charges against Paul had been dropped.

Relations among Native Americans and the rest of Americans have seldom been good and are not yet today. However, any of us who has lived the last seventy-five years can bear witness that there has been some progress made in our lifetime. The churches, including the ALC, have tried to play positive roles. I cannot foresee a future in which most American Indians can feel themselves genuinely at peace with the dominant majority of United States people. The relations will require constant work. The ALC has had a small role in building bridges rather than walls of hostility.

Racism

White racism has been an ugly blot on the United States throughout its history. Slavery, conflict, Civil War, reconstruction, poll tax, Ku Klux Klan, segregation, racial profiling—all describe the sorry history of white privilege and black suffering. All along the way there have been remarkable efforts at replacing racism with justice and peace for all. Committed racists have always found ways to thwart a single class citizenship. African Americans have been the primary victims, but there have been blatant episodes of white exploitation of Chinese, Japanese, Latin Americans, and others. The second half of the twentieth century was a time of racial turmoil in the U.S. It was also a time of major gains in the country's efforts to make good on its constitutional commitments to all American citizens. Official actions by the ALC during my lifetime have called for racial equality, but there was always a question as to the depth of individual commitment.

I had a lengthy history of opposition to racism and support for racial equality through my parish pastor days. That continued during my days as ALC president. During my years in office there were renewed racial peacemaking efforts by the ALC. Statements calling for racial justice were adopted by national and district conventions and by some congregations. Some of the statements were general, and some were very specific as, for instance, a statement calling for equal educational opportunity. More importantly there were increasing concrete actions aimed at ending racism. Many congregations in mixed racial neighborhoods took steps to become multi-racial. New congregations were started in communities of color where there were few if any Lutherans. Both the ALC national offices and ALC institutions actively recruited minority staff persons as well as board and committee members from those congregations. The result was a considerable number of very talented and capable staff persons who made lasting imprints on the lives of Lutherans who had previously had little contact with minority persons. It made a difference to have skilled minority educators leading large workshops on parish education or youth work or other parts of the church's work. Perhaps the most dramatic symbol of change in attitudes took place when Nelson Trout, an African-American, was elected bishop of the ALC South Pacific District.

Apartheid

ALC efforts for racial justice and peace were global in scope. The most significant illustration was in Southern Africa. The racist rigidity and cruel apartheid practices of the ruling white government in South Africa were increasingly condemned by churches and many governments throughout the Western world. The fact that the Dutch Reformed Church in South Africa was closely identified with the government and gave theological legitimacy to apartheid increased the concern of other Christian churches throughout the world.

The ALC had a century-long missionary history in South Africa. Toward the end of the nineteenth century, one of the ALC predecessor churches sent missionaries to join in work begun by missionaries from the Church of Norway. In the same era the Church of Finland began missionary witness in Namibia, which was also under the control of the government of South Africa. As a result of the missionary work, Lutheran churches with several hundred thousand members in each of the two countries became members of the Lutheran World Federation. Their requests for assistance came directly to the ALC and also to the LWF.

Initially the assistance sought from and given by the ALC was directed exclusively to the life and work of the Lutheran churches. During my years in office, the ALC became deeply involved on a broader front.

The ALC urged the U.S. government to impose sanctions on commerce with South Africa and to use U.S. influence with the government of South Africa. U.S. corporations were petitioned to use affirmative actions in support of the aspirations of black and colored people in South Africa. Some stockholder petitions were supported, and I met with major corporate heads to urge their company's support. Financial funding was provided for various South African initiatives, including funds for Nelson Mandela while he was still imprisoned on Robbins Island.

I made three trips to Southern Africa while in office, primarily as a way to indicate to the South African churches and to the South African government that the ALC and LWF were actively supporting the anti-apartheid cause in South Africa. The trips also allowed me to visit the ALC missionaries, seminary professors, and congregational pastors serving in Southern Africa. Our efforts were small by comparison with the need. We all knew, however, that it would only be through the cumulative power of many anti-apartheid interventions that success would finally come.

Two of the trips took me to both South Africa and Namibia. There were visits with lay and clergy in both countries as well as frequent opportunities to listen, preach, and worship. The show of solidarity from American churches was obviously encouraging to the people of the churches. President Marshall of the LCA and I spent a fruitful day negotiating with the managers of a very large British-owned copper mine in Namibia. A significant improvement in working conditions and a vastly improved housing program for native workers resulted. A lengthy visit with Dutch Reformed Pastor Beyers Naude of Johannesburg was inspiring. He was under house arrest for his outspoken opposition to the apartheid government. His opposition was especially important and influential, for he had been a major leader in the Dutch Reformed Church that was so closely allied with the apartheid government. He represented a crack in the apartheid wall.

Visits with Bishop Manas Buthelezi of Soweto, Bishops Auala and Dumeni in Namibia, and many of their constituents were inspiring because of their steadfast faith in Christ and the future in the face of constant threat.

One of my trips was made as a member of an LWF committee whose mandate was to see what progress three small, white Lutheran church bodies in Southern Africa were making toward uniting with surrounding black Lutheran church bodies. It was another way that Lutheran churches outside South Africa could bring witness to bear against apartheid. There was some progress but at a painfully slow pace.

Another trip took me to Harare, Zimbabwe, for a major meeting of Western church leaders called together by Archbishop Desmond Tutu of South Africa. The archbishop's role in South Africa has been heroic and crucial. The meeting provided opportunity for some who had been hesitant to become outspoken supporters of South African anti-apartheid efforts. A strong statement calling for the end of apartheid was made, and assurance was given of strong support for the anti-apartheid struggle in South Africa. The South African government frequently charged its opposition with being communist supported and controlled. The Harare meeting helped expose that as a blatant falsehood.

It is difficult to convey a sense of the importance black people in South Africa attached to such visitations from the churches of the West. They were often tempted to feel they were forgotten, unimportant, and impotent against the great military and political might of the apartheid regime. The presence of church leaders who came to assure them of the vigorous support of churches around the world helped sustain their hope for a better day ahead.

The same was true of invitations to Southern Africa church leaders to visit churches in the West. The ALC hosted several of them. Bishops Auala and Dumeni of Namibia spent quality time in the U.S., including at Luther Seminary in St. Paul. Volunteer American doctors provided prostate surgery for Bishop Auala and knee surgery for his wife, operations that were impossible for them in Namibia. Bishop Buthelezi, foremost Lutheran theologian in South Africa and often banned by the South African government, lectured at Lutheran seminaries in the U.S. Even though these African leaders discovered that racial prejudice still existed in the U.S., they also got a sense of the freedom that comes with U.S. citizenship and the remarkable changes occurring in the U.S.

The Environment

Environmental degradation was as great a threat to humanity as nuclear proliferation, though most of us were unaware of the magnitude of the environmental threat. Making peace with the environment should have been given as much or more attention as racism, the Cold War, or nuclear disarmament. However the churches, like most of society, were slow to see the extent of the threat to the environment. It was not that there was no awareness, but that it was too slow and too small. The ALC did speak in many ways of the responsibility of human beings to be God's stewards of the whole creation. The DLMC in 1978 issued a manual, *A Community of Stewards*, with many energy-conserving suggestions for congregations, colleges, nursing homes, and hospitals. The national offices took significant steps to lessen waste of energy resources.

The 1979 meeting at Camp David with President Carter spurred the churches to increased concern for environmental issues. At the meeting the major focus was on the necessity to reduce dependence on non-renewable energy sources, but the discussion ranged more widely to include the stewardship of the whole creation. The president made clear that he looked for the churches to call America to a higher environmental stewardship responsibility. We in turn had a variety of suggestions as to how the government could lead the way. As a result of the meeting I called for an ad hoc committee to develop an ALC plan for increasing environmental awareness. The following quote indicates the beginning usefulness of this committee:

> The first recommendations from the Energy Advisory Committee were received by the executive committee. David Rokke, staff person for the group, spoke enthusiastically of their first two meetings. As a result of the advisory committee's recommendation and Aid Association for Lutherans Insurance Company funding, the ALC will provide each congregation with two energy books. One is entitled *The Energy-efficient Church* and the other is a practical workbook entitled *Total Energy Management*, developed by National Electrical Contractors' Association and National Electrical Manufacturers Association. Further recommendations will be forthcoming.

The following 1979 quote from a speech to the LCMS convention is illustrative of the use of speaking opportunities to respond to the environmental crisis.

> We have been flirting with conservation for many years. Now it is time for deep seriousness. It is not just this moment's energy crisis that requires it. It is the underlying fact

that the sustainability of the earth and its people requires a moral commitment to conservation of all the earth's resources. Our responsibility is not only to this generation, else we will deserve the ugly title, "The Me Generation." Our responsibility is to this generation, and to our children's generation, and to our children's children's generation.

There were many specific things that the ALC did to heighten awareness of environmental needs. Important as the efforts were, however, they did not convey the urgency that is being displayed as I write this. For instance, the ALC exercised great concern for U.S. farm policy, but its primary aim was economic justice for farmers with the stewardship of the environment being secondary. Lutherans initiated extensive and excellent programs to improve agricultural practices in poor nations, but they were focused much more on food production than on paying urgent attention to responsibility for air, water, and earth.

While the ALC increasingly called for greater responsibility for the environment during my years in office, it did not receive the priority it deserved. I remember being asked in 1990, two years after leaving office, what the great public issue would be for the twenty-first century. By then I had seen and heard enough to answer, "The environment." In 1980, however, while environmental stewardship was seen in the church as a moral imperative, it was not given the attention we now know to be necessary.

Nobel Peace Prize Forum

A direct effort to encourage peacemaking by ALC college students is still going strong twenty years after its founding. In 1987 a friend, Mike Roan, called in my office and said he had just come from visiting his cousin, Jacob Sverdrup, in Oslo, Norway. Sverdrup was the director of the Nobel Institute which awards the annual Nobel Peace Prize. He had indicated a Nobel Institute interest in doing some kind of program on the American scene, especially among Scandinavian-American people in the U.S. Midwest.

Mike and I brainstormed and came up with the idea of annual Nobel Peace Prize Forums featuring Nobel Award winners. We thought the five Midwest colleges founded by Norwegian immigrants—Luther, Augsburg, St. Olaf, Concordia, and Augustana—might be interested in establishing Nobel Peace Prize Forums. I called President Sid Rand of St. Olaf College and asked for his opinion as to feasibility. He thought the idea had possibilities and should be presented to the five college presidents. The presidents liked the idea and agreed to a five-year cycle of forums with each of the colleges hosting one forum. The Norwegian Nobel Institute agreed to a working arrangement with the Peace Prize Forum and plans began to gel. In order to have some start-up money available I asked the ALC Board of Trustees for $10,000, and they made it available to the colleges.

The initiative came during my last year as ALC president. I was able to secure the interest of two prominent persons of Norwegian background, former U.S. Vice President Walter Mondale and former Governor Al Quie of Minnesota. Some kind of group had to be set up to administer the program, raise funds, and seek publicity. I chaired the group for the first several years after retiring as ALC president. Vice President Mondale proved especially valuable because of his access to Nobel laureates and other major U.S. and foreign political figures. Former St. Olaf College President Sidney Rand and former Minnesota Governor Al Quie were also most helpful in the early going. Their presence also made it relatively easy to recruit other board members. The participation of the Norwegian Nobel Institute was essential for success. We also received some funding and participation from a federally-funded U.S. Institute for Peace as well as from Northwest Airlines and Lutheran Brotherhood Fraternal Benefit Society.

The most important benefit of the forums has been the annual participation of 1500 to 2500 students from the five colleges. They have been able to declare their concern for peace as well as to listen to and interact with world leaders. College faculties and a goodly number of the general public have also participated. The first forum was in 1988 at St. Olaf College, and it was a huge success. The program featured Nobel Laureate Norman Borlaug of Green Revolution fame, and he was outstanding. Each of the subsequent nineteen forums has been inspiring.

As is most often the case, there is no way to establish how much the cause of peace has been affected by the Nobel Peace Prize Forums. It is possible to take heart that thousands of young college students have listened to and interacted with world renowned contributors to peace. There is no good alternative to pushing for peace. Those young college students will make their mark, and we have reason to hope they will help bless the world with peace.

CHAPTER 13

THE CHURCH AND THE COLD WAR

Both LWF and WCC churches had member churches and/or denominational partners in Eastern Europe. The Eastern European Lutherans have been referred to previously. The WCC included sizeable Reformed churches in East Germany, Hungary, Czechoslovakia, Poland, Yugoslavia, and Romania. The presence of the Orthodox churches in the WCC meant regular contact with the millions of Orthodox believers in the Soviet Union as well as Orthodox representatives from other Soviet bloc countries and the Middle East.

Ideological opposition, distrust, and Soviet tyranny created walls of separation that were rigidly enforced by the Soviet Union and its satellite countries. What started as a political and psychological wall took physical shape when the actual physical wall was built to separate East from West. The Iron Curtain effectively ended normal relations between peoples who shared common histories and, in millions of instances, common family ties. The churches became the only non-governmental organizations that were able to maintain some measure of meaningful contact across the Iron Curtain. They did so in a multitude of ways that were always difficult and sometimes dangerous.

The very fact that church representatives from both East and West were sometimes able to get visas and meet together was a significant peacemaking activity. Both LWF and WCC member churches existed across the East-West divide and were able in some instances to express fundamental Christian unity and make common cause in serving human needs. The meetings those groups held on both sides of the Iron Curtain illustrated to the wider society that people could live and work together peacefully in spite of widely differing political and cultural perspectives. Those of us from the West were able to see and feel the encouragement and hope that the meetings brought to our sister and brother Christians in the East.

Why the Soviet leadership allowed the churches some windows of opportunity was always an unanswered question. Nothing was certain. It seemed that visas were allowed or not allowed according to whims. Even those of us visiting from the West were always made to feel that we had no right to be there and were there by sufferance of the state. Yet there were extremely important cross-wall meetings of church people. The ties of friendship and sense of oneness in Christ stirred us from the West as much as it did those from the East.

LWF and WCC meetings enabled Western church leaders to meet with governmental officials of both East and West. The difference between East and West was acute. In the West the officials would listen and converse on important issues. You felt they were at least hearing your concerns. In the East the officials who met with groups of delegates would use most of the time to laud the Soviet Union as the agent of peace and blame the Western countries as the cause of international polarization. On a few occasions I did get Eastern political figures to dialogue about the merits of Soviet-style communism and Western capitalism. I always wondered how much the communists really believed and how much was a memorized litany that they were required to defend.

The Soviet system sought to bring everything, absolutely everything, under the control of the state. From the standpoint of Soviet leadership the churches, like everything else, belonged to the state and existed at the pleasure of the state. The state intended the churches to be subservient and used both sticks and carrots in the attempt to make that the reality. Even those of us visiting from the West were always made to feel we had no right to be there and were constantly watched by state agents.

My first meeting with church delegates from Eastern Europe provided me with a beginning understanding of the burdens placed on Eastern delegates to LWF and WCC. In 1970, while still vice president of the ALC, I attended the LWF international assembly in Evian, France. It was my first exposure to international church affairs. There were plenary sessions and then there were break-out small groups whose purpose was to discuss the issues raised in plenary. At the first two or three small group meetings I listened to delegates from the Eastern bloc cast the U.S. in negative terms. I was incensed at the one-sided criticism of the U.S. After a few such episodes I began making interventions defending the U.S. and criticizing the Soviets. After a day or two of this an East German theological professor asked if he could join me for lunch. When we had received our food he suggested we eat some distance from the dining hall on the beach of Lake Geneva where our conversation could be private. He then explained to me that I should take the anti-U.S. rhetoric with a grain of salt. Eastern delegates, by being mildly critical of the U.S. and avoiding anything negative about Soviet governments, would get a necessary positive report to the authorities back home. Without such reports it was a virtual certainty that they would come under suspicion and at the least would not be allowed to attend further meetings in the West. Delegates told us what a freeing, exhilarating experience it was to visit the West. What they considered to be mild criticism of the U.S. seemed to be a small price to pay, especially when they made certain those from the West knew what was happening. One could not help trying to minimize the danger for Eastern delegates. For some that meant giving the Soviet a free pass as far as criticism was concerned. I thought that understandable for delegates from the East, but counter-productive for those of us from the West.

My first meeting with the LWF executive committee was in Eisenach, East Germany, in 1973. I will not forget my anger and discomfort in the first moments behind the Iron Curtain. We were on a train from Frankfurt in West Germany to Eisenach in East Germany. The train stopped as soon as we crossed into East Germany, and my first sight out the window was of East German soldiers with their rifles and dogs apparently making sure nobody would detrain or cause any trouble. It was a grim way of letting us know that we were entering a different world.

The meeting in Eisenach was notable not least for its Cold War implications. The Iron Curtain had prevented any group meetings of East and West non-governmental personnel to that date. Eisenach, East Germany, so much a part of Martin Luther's life, was the site of the first large meeting of non-government personnel to be held in a country of the Soviet bloc. All of us were aware that it was a small breech in the wall separating people, a signal that peaceful intercourse could happen between the Eastern communist and Western capitalist worlds.

We arrived at Eisenach late in the evening and were taken to a fine old hotel owned by the Swedish Lutheran Church called Haus Heinstein. The noted Swedish Archbishop Söderblom had been responsible for the Swedish church purchasing it during the post-World War I years. When we awoke in the morning we looked out our window and had a breath-taking view of the Wartburg Castle, a Lutheran icon dating from Martin Luther's remarkable and productive stay 450 years earlier. The hotel was at the very base of the mountain and had been a Lutheran center for a century before our visit.

The contrasts between an oppressive, tyrannical state and a struggling church were always present. At the Eisenach meeting the East German minister of church affairs, a man named Ziggerwasser, hosted a dinner for the executive committee in the Wartburg Castle. In his speech he informed us, especially the East Germans, that we were most fortunate that the government was being so tolerant as to allow our meeting. He let us know in no uncertain terms that any trouble the churches caused would be dealt with "appropriately." It became a stirring occasion for me when the East German church respondent was equally clear in letting the minister know that while they sought to be peaceful citizens they also had to obey God rather than men. It was the first of many times that I heard the East German church leadership make clear their intention to be good citizens, but that their loyalty to God took precedence over their loyalty to the state. It was a brave stance to take, and many of the church leaders had to pay a hard price for their witness.

The Eisenach meeting was the first of many trips across the Iron Curtain into Eastern European countries for me. For a variety of ecumenical reasons, usually associated with the LWF or WCC, I traveled in Russia, Byelorussia, East Germany, Poland, Romania, and Hungary. It is hard to convey how important it was for people in repressive regimes to be visited by fellow believers from the free world. It gave oppressed people a sense of solidarity with and participation in a wider society than they could experience in their home countries. Oneness in Christ became alive as we worshipped and planned and discussed how we could help each other and reach out to the unbelieving world. It was humbling to be with a Latvian Lutheran bishop who had spent eleven years in Soviet gulags, or with an East German Lutheran leader whose brilliant children were not allowed to attend a university because, as he put it, "they had the wrong father." Openly professing Christians lived in daily awareness that they and their families and parishioners were vulnerable to the whims and judgments of officials whose stated goal was to eradicate the Christian faith. The Russian Orthodox faithful knew their governmental keepers had sent the vast majority of Russian Orthodox priests into gulags from which they never returned.

On a much lesser level it was a fearful time for those of us who visited in those countries. Even though we were approved visitors, we knew we were being under constant watch by government agents. The techniques of intimidation were legion. It began as soon as one set foot in an Eastern country. At Berlin's Checkpoint Charlie or an airport in Moscow or Warsaw or Budapest we were met at the customs desk with a distrusting, hostile stare that I cannot describe but which said you were an enemy. In the hotels in which we stayed there was a person on every floor whose duty it was to sit by the elevator, the only means of entrance and egress, and log when each person went in or out. We were told by Eastern counterparts to assume that our hotel rooms were bugged and that at each meeting there would be an intelligence agent who would be passing as a believer. I was warned by a Russian Orthodox delegate, for instance, that a particular high ranking Russian Orthodox official was a KGB agent. It was difficult to believe because he was kind and thoughtful, theologically astute, and to all outward appearances deeply engaged in the Orthodox faith. After the Soviet glasnost, however, he was identified from KGB records as a long-time agent. I prefer to believe that he was a double agent serving the church as well as the state.

It was always a question as to why the Soviet leaders allowed so many religious relationships and joint activity across the Iron Curtain. Our Russian Orthodox counterparts believed it was primarily to keep believers loyal to the state while the socialist dream gradually eliminated religious loyalties. The authorities had tried persecution. It caused more problems for the Soviet government than it cured. In addition Soviet leaders may have believed themselves and surely wanted the rest of the world to believe that socialism was the peace movement in the world. Certainly they wanted their own people to think so. Another cause for permission to meet across the wall was the hard currency that Western churches sent to assist the brethren in the East. West Germany sent huge sums of money to help sustain congregations in East Germany and elsewhere. The Scandinavian and American churches also financed many church initiatives behind the Iron Curtain. The Soviet governments badly needed hard currency, and they may have looked on allowing cross-cultural church relations as a cheap price to pay. Still another cause was the necessary role some of the churches played in the daily lives of people. I think especially of East Germany where the churches continued to operate the national health care system, a huge and vital operation. The hospitals and various other health agencies had been the responsibility of the churches for centuries. The East German government was always hard pressed for cash and, not wanting turmoil, found it easiest to let the church continue to run the health care system. Even so I remain surprised that the Soviets did not absolutely stop public religious expression and stop allowing LWF and WCC representatives to travel back and forth. There must have been other reasons I could not see.

My closest associations with persons from Eastern Europe were with Lutheran and Orthodox Christian believers. They were counterparts in the LWF and WCC, and I came to have the highest regard for most of them. The majority were sufficiently obedient to the state to stay out of trouble. However, they maintained the maximum degree of independence possible, and they looked and worked for the day when complete freedom of religion became the norm in their countries. They were the ones I most sought to support. It was such colleagues in East Germany who provided much of the leadership for the public social protests that ultimately brought down the repressive East German state. It was not accidental that it was from the churches that many thousands of people started their protest parades that triggered the collapse of the East German communist government.

There were a very few of the Christians who had embraced the socialist vision and were its ideological spokespersons. I was present when a church leader from India was awarded an Order of Lenin medal by a high government official in Moscow. In his response he declared that he had passionately embraced the Soviet revolution all his adult life. Most government supporters, however, believed that Soviet-style socialism was the reality, would be throughout their lifetime, and that Christian peoples' responsibility was to help make it the best possible social order. I thought their hopes naïve, though I could understand how they came to their point of view. I always sought to be civil and tried to assure them that our life in Christ was more important than our ideological biases.

The greatest difficulty for us Western Christians was to speak freely and forthrightly in our ecumenical meetings without getting our Eastern brothers and sisters in trouble. On various occasions I spoke critically of Soviet bloc policies. Soviet peoples were accustomed to criticism of the U.S. and had long since discounted that. They had not heard criticism of the Soviet bloc countries and, without saying so publicly, many found ways to let me know they were delighted with my words.

There were many wonderful stories describing the ways that Christian people thwarted the oppression behind the Iron Curtain. I will mention two that I thought remarkable, one in Romania and the other in Poland. Both of them involved the printing and distribution of Bibles. Both exploited a strange Soviet characteristic, namely, allowing opportunities that were not explicitly forbidden by the very rigid laws in existence.

In Romania the laws forbade the churches from purchasing printing presses. A LWF representative visiting the Orthodox church of Romania found that there was no law against receiving one as a gift. Returning to the LWF headquarters in Geneva he proposed that the LWF purchase a printing press and give it to the Romanian Orthodox church. As a result, in 1973 I stood alongside the Romanian Orthodox patriarch and watched the press pump out the pages that were to be bound into Bibles and New Testaments. The patriarch beamed as he thanked the LWF for the press and told us that to date it had enabled distribution of 240,000 New Testaments and 50,000 Bibles.

The Polish story is even more remarkable. Barbara Narzynski, wife of the Polish Lutheran bishop, managed a Christian bookstore in downtown Warsaw. I spent a day in the store watching in amazement as dozens of Polish people came in to purchase Bibles and other religious material. Mrs. Narzynski said they had been doing a land-office business for years and with delight told me how it was possible. The laws of Poland required the government printing office to meet an annual printing quota. Failure to meet a required quota in any of the Soviet countries was to guarantee dire results for the responsible officials. The government printing office was getting into a difficult squeeze because they could not obtain sufficient paper to meet their quota. Mrs. Narzynski talked with LWF officials from Sweden who agreed to provide her with large quantities of paper if she could use the paper for printing and distributing Christian materials including Bibles. Mrs. Narzynski made a proposal to the authorities, and they accepted. The upshot was that the government of Poland's printing office printed tens of thousands of Bibles and allowed their sale in order to meet their prescribed printing quotas. This was in a country where Bibles were forbidden. It is the kind of Alice in Wonderland story that kept cropping up in the hard-line Iron Curtain countries.

It is tempting to think the life of the churches played a crucial role in ending the Cold War. I settle for the conviction that the churches played an important role and that the open support of the Western churches was of great blessing to many.

Nuclear Disarmament

The threat of global nuclear war was constant during my years in office. The United States and the Soviet Union raced to keep up with each other in building arsenals. Each had the capacity to destroy not only the perceived enemy but the entire human race. Yet, still more nuclear bombs were being built. Each side built them long after there was any possibility of needing or using greater numbers of them. I have read convincing analyses of what would have happened if global war had occurred. The estimate was that 150 nuclear bombs would kill hundreds of millions people, inundate the world with radiation, and so devastate the infrastructure that survivors would struggle for existence at subsistence levels.

For many years peace was maintained because each side was faced by MAD, acronym for "mutually assured destruction." Each side in the Cold War thought it imperative to keep parity with the other in the building of more bombs. Each side was always certain that the other side had more bombs than they did and that more must be built to assure parity. Like most Americans, I believed in a strong United States military but thought the endless building of nuclear bombs was expensive and potentially catastrophic folly.

The Christian churches, called to be peacemakers, had to engage in efforts to dampen what was frequently referred to as "nuclear madness." The ALC, LWF, and WCC passed many resolutions regarding peacemaking, the Cold War, and nuclear disarmament. Members of the congregations were urged to pray and work for peace and the end of nuclear proliferation. There was always awareness that the churches did not offer any special foreign policy expertise, but there was also awareness that churches could not be silent in the face of possible nuclear war. The biblical call to peacemaking required the involvement of ALC people.

An indication of the ALC's attempt to support efforts for nuclear disarmament is evident in sentences from a letter I wrote to President Carter in 1979:

> The Church Council of the American Lutheran Church, meeting in Minneapolis, Minnesota, June 18-22, 1979, adopted resolutions which commend you, Mr. President, for your efforts in negotiating Salt II. . . . The council expresses gratitude to you for your persistent pursuit of a nuclear armament limitation treaty. We encourage you to lay plans for additional treaties even as the struggle for Salt II is in process.

I can be certain President Carter read the letter because he responded with a hand-written thank you note.

My role as ALC president provided opportunities to speak out in ways that I hoped would be helpful. I sought ways other than simply declaring opposition to nuclear proliferation. Occasionally there was an opportunity to publicly call for a unilateral action by either the U.S. or Soviet Union to reverse the proliferation of nuclear weapons. I supported the nuclear freeze movement that sought to have the two nuclear powers stop further production. Beyond that I urged the U.S. particularly to declare a cessation of bomb production with a challenge to the Soviet Union to follow suit. With the thousands of nuclear weapons already extant, it seemed to me no threat to the nuclear deterrent policy to make a unilateral halt in production for a specified period of time and challenge the Soviet Union to do the same. I believed the U.S. had to do everything prudent to stop the nuclear arms race. There was no question but that the large majority of ALC members joined me in praying for nuclear disarmament.

The attempt to support efforts to stop the incessant buildup of nuclear weapons was frustrating. Attempts to get the U.S. to initiate nuclear disarmament would evoke charges of being "soft on communism." In order to avoid such a taint I would declare in advance that I was militantly anti-communist, not a pacifist, and that I believed it necessary for the United States to seek peace through strength and not weakness. The proposed cessation of nuclear buildup with a challenge to the Soviet Union to do the same could then be offered as a possible policy. It never seemed to be taken seriously, however, though in retrospect it still seems sensible to me.

I recently read *Arsenals of Folly*, a book by Richard Rhodes. He uses copious quotes from recently released government documents to indicate how a strategically placed group of neo-conservatives (Cheney, Rumsfeld, Wolfowitz, Perle), the same group that urged President Bush to go to war in Iraq in 2003, were constantly urging President Reagan to continue the nuclear arms race well into the 1980s. The author's conclusion that these stockpiles of nuclear arms were "arsenals of folly" supports my strong feelings about them. The persistent production of nuclear arms had more to do with international paranoia than positive policy.

The single most important public statement I made in support of nuclear disarmament was in Moscow at a 1982 peace conference hosted by the Russian Orthodox Church. It seemed obvious to me that the Soviet government had given permission to the Russian Orthodox Church to hold the conference in order to use it for propaganda purposes. Even so, hosting the event was a very significant breakthrough for a Russian Orthodox Church that had previously known only enmity from the Soviet government. In order to give the conference legitimacy, Americans had to be included. The Orthodox leadership not only was able to include me as one of the delegates, but they also made me vice chair of a nine-member executive praesidium responsible for planning the meeting and arranging whatever follow-up there might be. Six hundred representatives from all major religions and all continents gathered for a week of meetings under the theme, "Religious Workers for Saving the Sacred Gift of Life from Nuclear Catastrophe."

I was appointed chairperson for the third major plenary meeting of the peace conference. The two previous plenary sessions had been marked by speeches that were highly political in substance, with the Soviet Union being lauded and the U.S. and its Western allies being blamed for fomenting the arms race. The evening before the third plenary meeting a group of LWF delegates met for an informal strategy session. We all agreed that something had to be done to change the tenor of the conference. With encouragement from others in the group, I decided to use my opportunity as chairperson to make a short statement. I include that statement in its entirety because there was wide agreement that it changed the character of the conference from that time forward. There were no more fawning speeches lauding the Soviets and damning the West.

> Let me begin this session by sharing one basic difficulty in taking this chair.

> This is my first visit to this hospitable country. I have come to participate in the endeavors for peace and to join in efforts to save the sacred gift of life from nuclear catastrophe. I thank Patriarch Pimen and the Russian Orthodox Church for attempting such a conference.

> I came as a disciple of Jesus Christ from the U.S.A. because I believed it possible that we could gather as religious people, people from many different religions, people whose highest loyalty is to the Almighty God, people who could rise above national, ideological, political, and religious dif-

ferences, and call all the peoples of the earth to stop the development of nuclear arms and begin the process of disarming.

My problem is that I believe this conference is in danger of becoming a political forum heavily tilted against the West. After the basically theological opening statements by Metropolitan Philaret and Patriarch Pimen, we have been treated mainly to a series of political speeches better suited for the United Nations. If we make of this conference a series of political charges and countercharges against West and East, we will go home with no great summons to the nations to rise above enmity and nuclear confrontation.

I therefore plead with you who will yet speak to do so out of religious conviction and to honor the principle of even-handedness. Do not send any delegate home to be asked why he or she did not respond in anger to the charges made against his or her country. If we are to do good, and I believe we can, it will be because we can speak a word together to all the nations of the world, a word that calls all peace-loving people to insist to all the nations of the world that humanity turn back from the development of nuclear arms and to universal peace.

When looking at this statement twenty-five years later it does not seem to be a big thing. Those who remember the height of the Cold War with its threatening polarization can appreciate that those words coming from an American at a religious meeting in Moscow was a big bombshell in churchly terms and a small bombshell in terms of the international politics of the day. I subsequently found out that the conference was carried live on the official Soviet television. People from East Germany and Hungary as well as Russia let me know they had been watching and listening and applauding. Even American network newscasts carried a brief sound bite of a portion of my statement.

The next day I was asked by a large delegation of journalists from many countries to appear at a press conference. Billy Graham had been at a similar press conference a day earlier and had commended the state of religious freedom in the Soviet Union. I was shocked that he had done so, though I subsequently learned that Graham was to lead evangelistic crusades in several Russian cities following the peace conference. I have no doubt he was trying to make sure that he gave the authorities no excuse for cancelling those events. When I was advised of what Graham had said and was asked similar questions by the reporters, I responded as strongly as I could. I remember saying that the state of religious freedom in the Soviet Union was terrible and that I hoped the peace conference was a sign that the Soviet government was moving away from religious repression and toward full religious freedom for its people. The journalists, mostly from the West, applauded.

The conference closed by publishing "An Appeal to Leaders and Followers of All Religions." It is a strong statement summoning all people to insist on the end of nuclear confrontation and threat of war. While it was not possible to make it a direct appeal to governments, the summons to "all" unmistakably includes governments. It is the nature of such group statements that they include too much and become too long. However, the call to enlist all people to oppose all development, testing, placing, and possible using of nuclear weapons by all peoples and nations is clear.

I believe the conference and concluding statement contributed to a rising tide of opposition to nuclear proliferation. For many of the 600 religious leaders it was the first time they had publicly called on their constituencies to oppose military nuclear build-up in their own and other countries. That the conference could meet in Moscow was of great significance. Looked at in retrospect, it certainly contributed to a marked change in Soviet attitudes toward religion. In previous years the Soviet government would not have allowed such a gathering to occur. It is never possible to know just how much effect such gatherings and appeals may have had. It is possible to know that it was the right kind of international ecumenical meeting at the right time.

That opinion was not shared by the U.S. State Department however. Avery Post, president of the United Church of Christ, Bill Thompson, stated clerk of the Presbyterian Church USA, and I were invited to report to the State Department on our Moscow experience. First we met with Hugh Simon, an undersecretary for Soviet affairs, and George Lister, long-time Soviet specialist. They thought we had served Soviet policy goals by participating in the peace conference. I quote from my July 1983 *The Month That Was:*

We gave a number of reasons why we thought we served American interests and especially Christian interests. They acknowledged we had given the conference a different tone than it otherwise would have had. They also acknowledged that we had a responsibility to share the difficulty of life with Eastern Christians and could not look simply upon ourselves as instruments of U.S. foreign policy. That we were not in the State Department doghouse became apparent both from the conversation and also by the request that we return for a meeting with Deputy Secretary for Human Rights Elliott Abrams. The agenda is to be broad-ranging including Central America and other world areas.

An important by-product was the ecumenical solidarity, mutual respect, and meaningful friendships that marked the associations between Orthodox and Protestant Christians. While not exactly pertinent to a discussion on nuclear disarmament, I believe such friendships and associations, when multiplied many times, had a positive effect on subsequent meetings of people from East and West. I cite three personal experiences as evidence of a changing mood. I think they are indications of the importance of non-governmental meetings across the Iron Curtain.

A follow-up meeting of the conference praesidium was held in January 1983. Metropolitan Philaret, chair of the peace conference, head of the Russian Orthodox ecumenical relations office, and most powerful person in the Russian Orthodox Church hierarchy, invited Ann and me to come three days early and celebrate the Russian Orthodox Christmas with him in his diocese in Minsk.

The public character of our visit became evident when a very large gathering was assembled at the city's largest hotel for a celebration where we were honored guests. In order to emphasize its non-religious character, still a necessity in the anti-religious Soviet Union, the party centered on the arrival of "Father Christmas and the Snow Maiden" with gifts for all. The mayor and other public officials were present. They politely welcomed us and then gave their pro-forma speeches about the great accomplishments of the Soviet Union. In my response I emphasized the great desire of American people for friendly and peaceful relations with Soviet people. The obvious desire of the people to reach out to us, public officials included, was an indication of their desire to bring a new day to international relations.

The religious character of our visit was emphasized with our attendance at two Christmas worship services in the great Minsk cathedral. Ann and I were ushered to the front of the church and introduced as brother and sister Christians. A bench was placed behind us so that we could sit for a part of the time. There are no pews in Orthodox churches, so the faithful have to stand throughout the three-hour service. The first service started at 7:00 p.m. and the second at 2:00 a.m.! Both services were packed with people. At 5:00 a.m., following the second service, a Christmas feast was prepared by an order of Orthodox nuns and served in the metropolitan's adjacent residence. The feast's high point for me came with the dessert. The metropolitan announced that the nuns had created a new ice cream and named it "Ice Cream David Preus." Russian ice cream is extraordinarily good, and the metropolitan had observed my enjoyment of it at meetings in Moscow. I mention this as an instance of the many little and big ways that attention was called to the close relations not only between us personally but as representatives of church and nation.

A second remarkable event was a five-day visit as guests of Metropolitan David of Soviet Georgia. The metropolitan and I became friends through service on the WCC Central Committee. He made a ritual at each meeting of rushing up to me, embracing me, and turning to whoever was nearby, saying in a loud voice while pointing first to me and then to himself, "David, David—brothers!" It exhausted his English, but it communicated the importance of both Soviet-American and Lutheran-Orthodox associations.

There were many high points during this visit. I will mention the most public one. Metropolitan David had arranged for me to be awarded the Georgian Orthodox Church's St. George Medal. The Orthodox Church hosted several hundred people for dinner in Sukhumi, a large city on the Black Sea famous for its outstanding research university. Notables from city, state, and university, as well as outstanding artists and musicians were introduced as honored guests. Then came the award ceremony followed by many toasts using great ram-horns drinking flagons. Most of the toasts were about enduring Georgian-American friendship. The Georgians could not say it in so many words, but it was obvious that they were making a statement against continuation of the U.S.-Soviet nuclear stand-off. Metropolitan David also made sure that everybody also knew that the event was a sign of Orthodox-Lutheran unity in Christ as well as a sign of friendship between Georgia and the United States.

The third illustration occurred at a meeting of the WCC Central Committee in Geneva, Switzerland. A new Central Committee moderator, the chief elected officer of the Central Committee, was to be chosen. Metropolitan Philaret, who had served on the search committee, told me afterward that the Orthodox had put my name forward. He was confident that I would have been elected except for a provision that candidates must have the support of their home country's delegations. Other members of the American delegation were representing the U.S. National Council of Churches as well as their denominations. They thought it would be impossible to elect as moderator of the World Council a delegate whose church did not belong to the U.S. National Council. A German Lutheran delegate was subsequently elected. It was good for my sake that the Orthodox move did not succeed. However, I think the support of the Orthodox was positive and moving and indicative of the strength of common Christian faith and friendship. It was notable, too, as a way of reaching across the East-West divide. I also thought the action of the Americans from the National Council of Churches was understandable and sensible.

At the time I was surprised and pleased that such events could take place. In retrospect I see them as signs of a thawing in the Soviet attitudes toward the West. *Glasnost* and *perestroika* were in their early stages, but those of us from the West did not know it. We could only rejoice that such signs of East-West friendship were now being allowed. It also indicated the importance of the WCC and LWF in enabling people to break down the walls of separation between both religious and political entities. It is my belief that the multiplication of such small events is important in making it possible for political leaders to make peace between nations.

One other interesting Moscow experience deserves to be mentioned. *Glasnost* was becoming publicly known toward the end of the 1980s. Attitudes were changing. The WCC Central Committee was invited to hold its 1987 meeting in Moscow. The Russian government welcomed us with a lavish reception in the Kremlin. It was held in the great hall which was built by the tsars and used for seventy years as the meeting place of the Communist Internationale. It was a stunning experience, not only because we were being received by the Russian government, but also because of the huge number of Christian symbols built into the building. In thousands of churches and other places the Soviet officials had gone to great lengths to obliterate Christian symbolism. Here at the central meeting place of the Communist Party were dozens of crosses built into the very walls of the meeting hall. We were told that at the time of the 1917 revolution Lenin had forbidden any desecration of the Kremlin buildings. He declared that they were treasures that belonged to all the Russian people. We also toured the tsarina's spacious apartment in the Kremlin. It was virtually a Christian art gallery. I still wonder whether the extensive Christian symbolism in so much of the Kremlin affected the private thoughts of Soviet leaders.

I had other involvements aimed at nuclear disarmament and associated important human rights problems. In 1978 President Carter appointed me to be one of eight public advisors to the U.S. representatives on the Council on Security and Cooperation in Europe (CSCE). Wide ranging East-West agreements on what came to be known as the Helsinki Agreements represented an important advance in relationships. The signatory countries agreed to establish CSCE meetings to regularly assess and encourage implementation of the agreements. The permanent U.S. delegates were Ambassador Kampelman and Judge Bell, two prominent persons in the administration of President Jimmy Carter. At each CSCE meeting there were public advisors who were appointed by the president to observe the proceedings for two weeks and then make observations and recommendations to the permanent representatives. I was one of the group appointed in 1978. I thought it significant that one who had been urging nuclear disarmament initiatives should be included in the delegation.

During those two weeks I had to keep reminding myself that the Soviet Union had actually signed the Helsinki Agreements. Observing the plenary sessions made clear that the Soviet representatives had instructions to stall, criticize, and obfuscate the proceedings. For instance, the agreements called for each signatory nation to identify human rights failures in their own country and indicate what steps were being taken to address them. Western countries honestly reported their shortcomings and their attempts to alleviate them. All Soviet bloc country spokespersons refused to acknowledge any human rights violations in their countries. When their representatives spoke, they used the time to flay the Western countries for their failures and to ridicule them for failing to adequately address their problems. It was obvious there was no intent to let the Helsinki Agreements actually affect Soviet thinking and acting.

Yet they had voted for the agreements. A standard had been set. It was possible to keep pointing to an agreement the Soviets had signed. The outline of a way to begin moving from nuclear confrontation to nuclear disarmament had been signed. The meetings had to go on as a way of undergirding the agreements that had been reached. The hope was that patient pursuit of the Helsinki goals would help produce a change in Soviet attitudes and practices. Such was our counsel as advisors.

Again it was an opportunity for human interchange between peoples. People from East and West would eat meals with each other and engage in discussions. Once outside the formal meetings, it was possible to talk as neighbors rather than as officials. It provided opportunities for peoples from East and West to spend time together, to socialize and to recognize that it was useless to demonize each other. It was another of the countless small engagements that helped create a climate for change.

In 1982 a discussion on nuclear policy and human rights was held at the State Department. Participants were Secretary for Human Rights Elliott Abrams; Admiral Howe, director of the Arms Control and Disarmament Agency; his second in command, Joe Lehman; Michael Novak from the Human Rights Commission; and several of Secretary Abrams' staff. Bill Thompson and Jim Andrews (Presbyterian), Arie Brouwer (Reformed), James Crumley and I (Lutheran) were joined by Alan Geyer of the Center for Theology and Public Policy. I quote from *The Month That Was*, October 1982:

> The church leaders indicated a dubious attitude toward the Reagan disarmament initiatives. We suggested they were so pro-U.S. tilted that the Soviets could not take them seriously. We suspected they were more for U.S. political consumption than for serious negotiations. The State Department people responded that the Soviets were taking them seriously, and it ill behooved Americans to do less. That was a pretty good stopper.

The trouble was that the Soviets were "taking them seriously" by building more bombs.

During the years of 1975 through 1987 I had many opportunities to express strong support for nuclear disarmament to high government officials. I had private conversations either by myself or with one or two other church leaders with five U.S. secretaries of state—Muskie, Vance, Rusk, Haig, and Schultz—during my years as ALC president. They talked with me because I was president of a major U.S. church body and an officer of the LWF and WCC. I was able to address the church's concern about racism in South Africa and nuclear proliferation, and make my personal plea that the U.S. initiate a radical plan for nuclear disarmament. There were no indications that my efforts had any effect, but at least it added another voice to a widespread concern.

I was invited to a couple of briefings in Washington in the White House or State Department, but they were informational meetings designed to show why nuclear arms were crucial and necessary. On another occasion I was invited to dinner and conversation at the Pentagon with the then-U.S. Secretary of Defense Cap Weinberger. There were only about a dozen of us outsiders included, and it was a fascinating evening, though the idea that it was a conversation was hardly the case. A couple of four-star generals were there, and by the time Weinberger and the generals finished telling us all the reasons why the U.S. needed to continue expanding its military and nuclear prowess there was little time left for the rest of us to speak. There was no explanation as to why I was invited. However, it must have had to do with my being president of a major U.S. church and an advocate for nuclear disarmament.

Speaking for nuclear peace also took me outside the U.S. The Evangelical Churches of West Germany brought together in Tutzing a body of representatives from both East and West to address nuclear disarmament in general and also the imminent threat to Europe by the placement of armed nuclear missiles near the wall separating East and West. The symposium was fascinating. The State Departments of the U.S., Soviet Union, and West Germany participated with about eight to twelve government officials apiece. I was invited to be one of the speakers as well as participant in the three-day meeting. Again I thought it valuable in building strong, insistent support for movement toward nuclear disarmament. The public sessions were much like the Helsinki follow-up meetings in Madrid. Charges and counter-charges were made, with the Soviets insisting they were faultless. However, the private conversation during breaks and at mealtimes was another matter. At dinner one evening I sat with the West German and Soviet heads of delegations as they talked very frankly about the possibility of reducing tensions over Soviet missile placements in Germany.

After the Tutzing meeting I was invited by Lutheran Bishop Hansel-mann of Bavaria to address a large gathering of youth peace advocates. They packed a very large auditorium in Munich and were highly agitated that Germany was again threatened with war. The placement of missiles and the massing of military forces on both sides of the Iron Curtain had them fearful and angry. They listened to me politely, but they clearly wanted something much more dramatic than I could give them. I urged limited unilateral disarmament actions by the West, accompanied by challenges to the East to do likewise. The youth saw that as a gradualist kind of approach. They were looking for something much more dramat-ic, something that would quickly produce an end to the military threat, and something they could help bring about that would produce some immediate results.

The ALC had no direct responsibility for the nuclear threat or the Cold War or the international peace process. U.S. political decisions are ultimately the result of the collective will of a free democratic public that is informed by free discussion. Church leaders were free to speak their minds about peace, and they did. I was able to be the church's public voice in many settings. Whether those representations were im-portant or not is impossible to know. It is the case that both Russia and the United States have destroyed thousands of nuclear bombs and have agreements to continue reducing the numbers. The nuclear threat remains with us, however, and it seems likely it will always be present as a threat to humanity. We can know that the church spoke out against nuclear proliferation and for nuclear disarmament. We used what we had—our voice. It was the responsible thing to do.

CHAPTER 14

CONCLUDING REFLECTIONS

My greatest personal satisfaction from my years as church body president is that the ALC stayed solid, strong, and enthusiastic in faith and mission through troubled and challenging years. The ALC kept the focus on God and the gospel. At the beginning of this book I cited my four priorities as evangelism, congregations, unity, and justice. What follows is my estimate of the work accomplished in those areas during my term in office.

Evangelism

There was never any question as to the centrality of evangelism in the life of the American Lutheran Church. The understanding was clear and deep that the church was tirelessly, ceaselessly, and enthusiastically to bear witness to the power and love of the Triune God. Though engaged in a varied host of ministries, ALC people knew themselves to be evangelical and Lutheran in all their ministries. The solid doctrinal clarity of Lutheran teaching and preaching made certain that Lutherans did not stray from the gospel core. The centrality of evangelism was never in question. That was case when I took office, and it was the case as I left.

Evangelism needs to be understood in two ways. One is the intentional evangelism where believers preach and teach the gospel in order that others may come to faith in Christ. It is the immediate response to God's charge, "Go, make disciples of all nations." It is the verbal declaration of the gospel with the prayerful intent that others may believe. All believers are urged to be personal evangelists.

The other understanding is that everything that is done in response to God is witness to God; it is evangelism and may be the spark that ignites faith in human hearts. Sturdy faith in God, loyal participation in congregational worship and work, and living witness to the lordship of Christ in all of life has been the best kind of Lutheran evangelism. Neighbors and friends know when people practice their faith. Lutherans are at their best in evangelism when they reach out to others and invite them to participate in congregational worship and service. Outstanding educational efforts, Bible studies, youth work, stirring music and worship, plus the certainty of gospel preaching has attracted significant numbers of Americans to life in Christ in ALC congregations. So have the many ministries the churches have initiated and sustained for human good, especially ministries for the world's poor. It is true that the Christian faith is "caught" as well as "taught."

American Lutherans generally know they have an evangelism responsibility. They take that responsibility seriously and enthusiastically in their support of global and American missions. It was always a joy for me to report on the amazing growth of indigenous churches that grew out of missionary evangelism around the world. It was equally exciting to tell of the evangelical outreach that has accompanied the start-up of new congregations in the U.S. While not very confident of their personal evangelism, ALC members have been very forth-coming in support of world and American missions.

Evangelism was always a major priority during my years of service. That was not a new thing for Lutherans, but it was a faithful continuation of a consistent core concern for Lutherans. Our generation sustained the priority.

Congregations

ALC congregations were united in essentials. In most congregations the esprit remained high. Groups of Christ's followers gathered in local settings to worship God and bear one another's burdens. They united in embracing the evangelical Lutheran Confessions. Word and Sacrament held central place in congregational life. Parishioners confessed their sins and looked to the crucified and risen Christ for forgiveness. They sought to serve God and God's people. They established various church bodies and councils to express their unity with other Christians, and to extend the gospel ministry throughout the neighborhood, nation, and world. Those facts were sources of great encouragement, and they made possible hopefulness for the future. I believe the ALC was a strong church body with remarkably good spirit because it was formed and sustained by strong congregations.

But all was not quiet and peaceful and easy for the congregations. They existed in vastly different settings, some easier for gospel ministry and some much harder. ALC congregations, their pastors, and their national staff struggled to meet the many challenges. The majority of ALC congregations were in small towns and open country where out-migration was intense, especially among young people. It was hard to keep the spirit strong in the face of dwindling numbers of parishioners. Inner cities had plenty of people, but the neighborhoods became poorer and poorer, and new immigrants had differing religions, languages, and cultures. Even in communities of affluence American culture provided endless diversions, and it was very easy to be distracted from serious discipleship. Challenges abounded in all American neighborhoods.

The congregation as the basic manifestation of Christ's church was taken for granted during my years as ALC president. So was the ALC constitutional definition of the ALC as a "union of congregations."

I frequently referred to the national and district offices as "extended arms of the congregations." In the main, ALC people in the local congregations knew the ALC's extended mission was initiated by the congregations and could only continue with their support. The national and district personnel knew themselves to be servants of the congregations.

Helping the congregations of the ALC to equip their members for twentieth-century Christian mission was a major responsibility for the ALC national boards and offices. The service provided by the ALC national offices was always good and sometimes brilliant. Complaints came because there was "not enough" of a particular program. Seldom was there criticism of the content or quality of the services.

Congregational satisfaction with and interest in ALC global and American missions was always at a high level. Gratitude for and trust in the seminaries and colleges was evident in the support they received. Social service ministries were outstanding, with a strong local "hands on" character that was much appreciated. Congregations believed they were well served by the national offices responsible for those ministries, and they showed it with consistently high interest and strong financial support.

The American Lutheran Church maintained its evangelical centrality and enthusiasm, was engaged in doing a host of good works, and was making major contributions to the unity of Christ's church throughout my term. The congregations, for all their challenges, were of positive and good spirit.

Unity

Significant contributions to the unity of the church were made during my pastoral and presidential years. At First Lutheran Church in Brookings, South Dakota; Trinity Lutheran Church in Vermillion, South Dakota; and the University Lutheran Church of Hope in Minneapolis, diverse memberships of laboring people, university students and faculty, homemakers, professional and business people, with a significant mixture of differing races and new immigrants, formed faithful, spirited, and mission-minded congregations. American Lutheran Church congregations' relations with other neighborhood congregations were generally excellent, and the congregations were important contributors to the unity of churches, neighborhoods, and cities.

The unity of the ALC was consistent and strong even at a time of widespread social unrest. There was theological variety within the ALC, but the different points of view were within the boundaries of the Lutheran Confessions. Significant differences on important social issues such as the Vietnam War, apartheid, and abortion were dealt with without breaking the unity. Differences in attitudes toward merging with the LCA and AELC were aired and brought to vote, decided, and entered, with a very small minority leaving the ALC fellowship. ALC participation in councils of churches at local, national, and international levels was testimony to ALC life in the one church of Christ

Unity in the church is both a given and a goal. God gives the church its unity. Christians are inextricably bound together as believers in the Triune God. God breathes faith into our hearts and makes us members together in the body of Christ. At the same time believers are called to practice the given unity as a life-long goal. The hospitality and friendship of the laity from many different church bodies constantly deepened during my years of service. In like manner my understanding and practice of unity grew in depth and intensity throughout my adult life. My greatest contributions to the cause of unity came in joint expressions of faith, hope, and love with a wide range of believers from many sectors of the church. Protestants of many confessions, Roman Catholics of many orders, Orthodox in their ethnic varieties—we found faith in Christ binding us together. As I said earlier, the daily neighborhood expressions of unity in Christ increased dramatically during my lifetime.

Human differences, even confessional differences, exist for Christians living in reconciled diversity. I do not know where this term originated, but it provides language for the unity of followers of Christ across a wide spectrum of doctrine and practice. The church is one in Christ in a unity given by God even as believers still strive to express that unity in the face of significant differences.

Throughout my years as church president I was steadily and increasingly aware of God's call to unity in the church, in society, and in the whole creation. I believe this awareness was shared and grew throughout the ALC. The need to express the measure of unity that exists in churches and society becomes increasingly important as the threats to human and global futures become more dangerous.

Justice

The major ALC work in support of justice was in the parishes. The national offices assisted by providing educational materials and in reports and sermons by staff. As church president I was able to be a strong voice for justice in many settings. It was a matter of setting a tone throughout the church, and I believe there was a marked strengthening in commitment to doing justice throughout the ALC during my years of service. As mentioned earlier, the ALC in a variety of ways addressed such issues as racism, sexism, apartheid, nuclear disarmament, torture, and war. The congregations and clergy sought to have an effect in these areas while keeping the primary focus on the grace of God that frees humans from sin and death no matter what the earthly future brings.

The separation of church and state is a great treasure and was consistently supported in the ALC. Congregations and the church body urged good citizenship as a part of Christian life and responsibility. At the same time churches maintained their independence from state domination. There was increased awareness that Christian people and congregations ought to applaud public actions that are just and criticize public actions that are unjust. The American Lutheran Church counted life in the United States a blessing and found many ways to say so without becoming servile or quiescent.

Dialogue between representatives of the church with representatives of the state increased significantly during my years in office. Awareness of the high moral content of many governmental responsibilities made governmental leaders open to the opinions of churches and church leaders as well as to the general public. The ALC sought to provide its membership with thoughtful studies on difficult public issues. The hope was that an informed membership would make positive contribution to public discourse and just actions on particular issues.

The ALC's actions for justice were strong without dominating ALC evangelical life and work. It is impossible to measure how much good resulted from church efforts in behalf of justice. It is enough that the ALC made heartfelt effort to obediently "do justice, love kindness, and walk humbly with God."

The ALC stayed strong throughout my years in office. I take great encouragement from that. Public society was troubled. Churches had to prove their faithfulness to the gospel and their adequacy in expounding it in the face of heavy criticism. The ALC made positive contributions to public society even as it grew stronger in its internal life.

The ALC held to its strong tradition in evangelism. ALC congregations maintained strong Word and Sacrament ministries while reaching out in myriad ministries. ALC unity was affirmed even in the midst of contentious issues, and the ALC reached out in many ways to express unity with other churches and the entire society. The ALC was committed to doing justice and to supporting justice in local communities, in states and nations, and in the whole creation. I believe the ALC made good on its God-given priorities. I left office convinced that the ALC had been a faithful and productive servant of God.

Gratitude

Gratitude is the one word that best describes my feelings when looking back on my thirty-eight years of pastoral service in the ELC and ALC. The grace of God has been an unfailing source of strength and hope. God has opened the doors in wonderful ways for me to preach and teach the gospel of Christ and has provided endless opportunities to serve God's people. I believe my ministry has been of some use in many of the areas described in this book. The people of the American Lutheran Church consistently welcomed me with gracious love and encouragement. Enriching friendships with so many grand people have been a great source of strength and pleasure. The marvelous variety of people and experiences in so many parts of the planet have been an unexpected bonus. My wife, Ann, has been a constant source of support, a wonderful partner, a wise counselor, a great mother for our children, and an unfailing source of love and fun. Our children made home a place of joy and supported me unfailingly when it would have been easy to find fault. Looking back, I am awed that through the years the grace of God, the love of Christ, and the unity born of the Spirit have become for me steadily richer and deeper.

I am blessed beyond reason and look to the future with hope.

Soli Deo Gloria!

PHOTOS

Basketball team at Luther College, Decorah, Iowa. Preus, front row center, is holding the ball.

In the pulpit at University Lutheran Church of Hope, Minneapolis, where Preus served from 1958 to 1973.

Preus chairing the Minneapolis School Board.

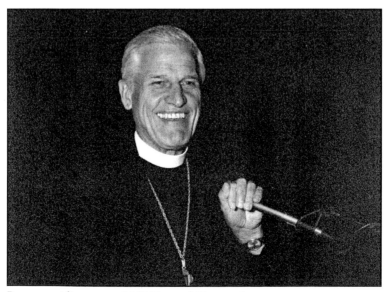

Preus presiding at an ALC General Convention.

ALC Vice President Fred Meuser and his wife, Jeanne, with Ann and David Preus, relaxing after an ALC Convention plenary.

ALC officers, General Secretary Arnold Mickelson, Vice President Lloyd Svendsbye, and President David Preus, at the 1980 ALC General Convention.

Preus welcoming Pastor Martin Luther King Sr. to speak at the 1974 ALC General Convention in Detroit.

King Olaf of Norway and Preus following worship at Ballard First Lutheran Church in Seattle, Washington.

Pope John Paul II and Vatican Secretary for Christian Unity, Cardinal Willebrands, with Preus following a personal meeting with the pope.

Preus with African and Orthodox church leaders at a World Council of Churches executive committee meeting.

Preus, vice chair of the 1982 Moscow Peace Conference, with the Reverend Billy Graham.

ALC delegation to WCC Assembly, Nairobi, Kenya, in 1975—Back row: Warren Quanbeck, Morris Sorenson, David Preus, Carl Mau, Willmar Thorkelson. Middle row: James Long, Margaret Bauman, Mr. Bauman, Arnold Mickelson, William Billings. Front row: Dagmar Quanbeck, Mrs. Hill, Margaret Youngquist, Marjorie Mickelson, Mrs. Thorkelson.

Preparing to process for a service of Holy Communion at a national convention of American Lutheran Church Women, with Preus as the presiding minister.

Newly-elected national officers of the American Lutheran Church Women in San Antonio: Fern Gudmestad, president; LaVonne Droemer, first vice president; Wilma Pierson, second vice president, being installed by Preus.

Clyde Bellecourt, American Indian Movement leader, talking with Preus after the standoff with U.S. marshals at Wounded Knee, South Dakota.

Bishop Josiah Kibira, LWF president from 1977 to 1985, with Ann and David Preus.

Former U.S. President Jimmy Carter and Mrs. Carter with Preus.

Ann and David with former U.S. Vice President Walter Mondale and Mrs. Mondale at Preus' retirement dinner.

Ann and David Preus in Kyoto, Japan. Photo by missionary John DeYoung.

Ann and David Preus family at retirement party—Back row: Stephen and David A. Preus. Middle row: Mrs. Stephen (Martha Olstad) Preus, Martha Kristine Preus, Mrs. David A. (Carmenza Duque) Preus. Front row: Louise Preus Parish, David and Ann, Laura Preus.